Introduction to Digital Media for Designers and Artists

Jim Jeffers, M.A., M.F.A.
Indian River State College

Kendall Hunt
publishing company

Cover image and all interior illustrations and photos courtesy of Jim Jeffers, unless otherwise noted.

Kendall Hunt
publishing company

www.kendallhunt.com
Send all inquiries to:
4050 Westmark Drive
Dubuque, IA 52004-1840

Copyright © 2017 by Kendall Hunt Publishing Company

ISBN 978-1-5249-3381-4

All rights reserved. No part of this publication may be reproduced, stored in a retrieval system, or transmitted, in any form or by any means, electronic, mechanical, photocopying, recording, or otherwise, without the prior written permission of the copyright owner.

Published in the United States of America

CONTENTS

About the Author   v
Acknowledgments   vii
Introduction   ix

PART 1: IMAGE CREATION AND EDITING SOFTWARE BASICS—LEARNING TO FISH RATHER THAN BEING GIVEN A FISH   1

Chapter 1: What Is Digital Media?   3
    Analog versus Digital   4
    The Computer as a Tool   5
    Intellectual Curiosity   6

Chapter 2: Application Basics   7
    Mac OS Key Features   7
    Disclosure Triangles, Hamburger Menus, and Timeless Tools   8
    Understanding Context and Visual Cues   9
    The Basic Ideas of Digital Media Applications   11
    Adobe Photoshop   20
    Adobe Illustrator   22
    Adobe InDesign   24

Chapter 3: Why Do I Need to Know This Stuff? 39
    How We Use Files across Applications 39
    Basic 3D 41
    Video, Animation, and Effects Software 42

PART 2: DESIGN BASICS: LEARNING TO SEE AGAIN 45

Chapter 4: Art and Design 47
    What Is the Difference between Art and Design? 47
    The Graphic Design Process 50
    Design in All Things 54

Chapter 5: The Fundamental Elements 59
    Line 60
    Shape 61
    Form 66
    Color 68
    Color Schemes 74
    Texture 78
    Space 79

Chapter 6: Compositional Ideas and Design Principles 87
    Compositional Ideas 88
    Abstraction 90
    The Symbol 91
    Design Principles 92
    Thoughts on Rules in Design and Art 102

Chapter 7: Helpful Information 103
    The Size of Things 103
    Typography Basics 108
    Printing 125
    Web Design 130

Introduction to Digital Media for Designers and Artists

About the Author

Artist, designer, educator, father, Jim Jeffers works with computer mediation, Web art, performance, photography, and video in conjunction with conventional media. Exploring cultural material and material culture, Jeffers is interested in most things, particularly superheroes, airplanes, car design, Swiss Army knives, rabbits, the new age of amazing television, good design in all things, and global fairness. His work has been exhibited nationally and internationally in over 80 exhibitions. In his nearly two decades of teaching, Jim has taught over 150 classes, and hundreds of students. He holds degrees from the University of California–Santa Cruz, New York University, and a Master of Fine Arts degree from Rutgers University. He has served on the boards of many non-profit arts organizations, most notably the New Media Caucus, where, as a founding member of the organization, he currently serves as the treasurer. Jim teaches at Indian River State College in Fort Pierce, Florida.

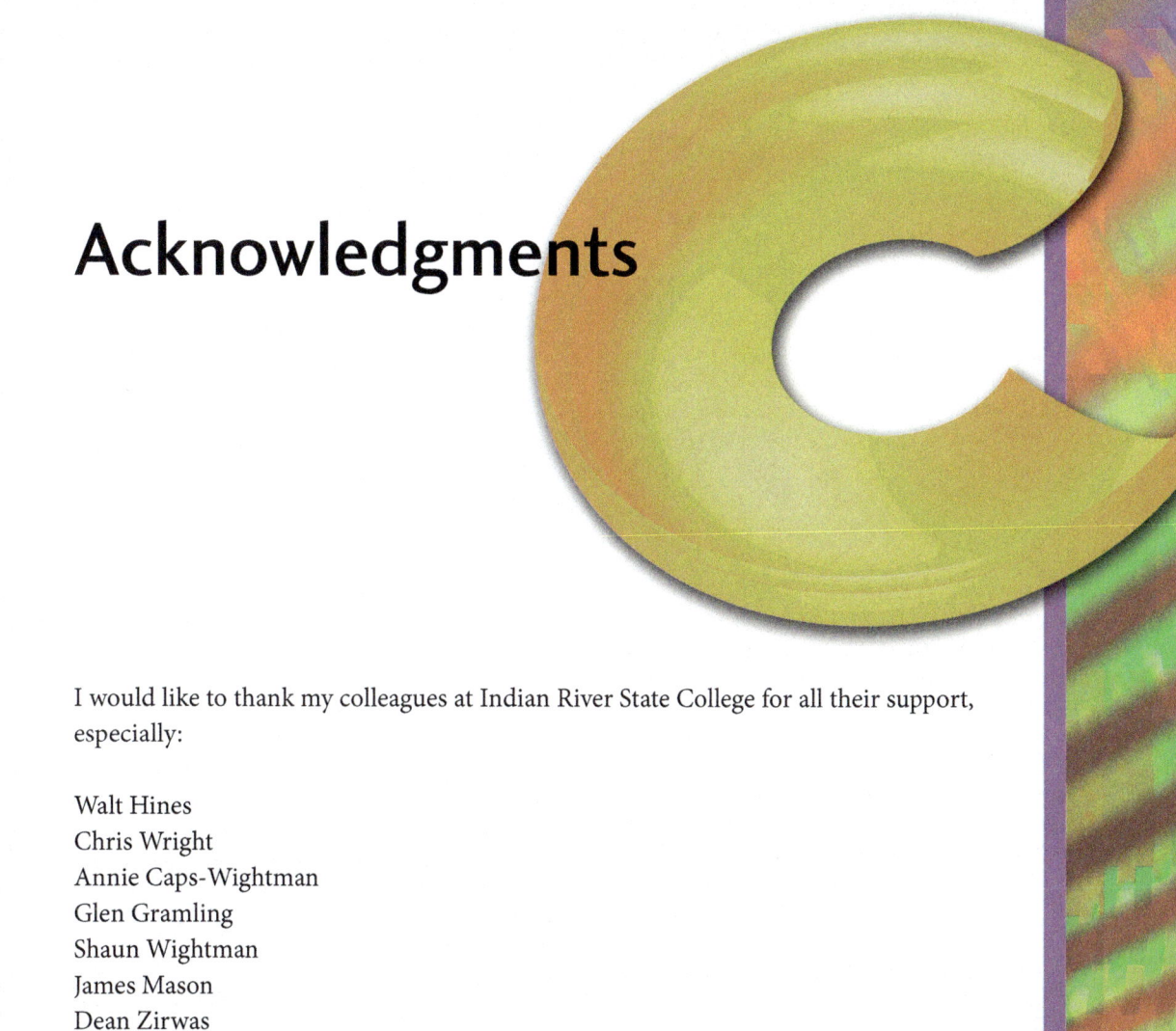

Acknowledgments

I would like to thank my colleagues at Indian River State College for all their support, especially:

Walt Hines
Chris Wright
Annie Caps-Wightman
Glen Gramling
Shaun Wightman
James Mason
Dean Zirwas
Gary Koser
Kevin Cooper

Introduction

Being an educator for nearly two decades, I yearned for a book with the answers to the day-to-day questions I am asked most in the classroom, and a book with the basics all designers and artists should know before going out into the world. This is the book I hoped for with the important information for designers and artists in the 21st century, where computers of all shapes and sizes dominate the teaching, learning, and working landscape. In explaining the interface, strategies, and general workflow of the digital age of art-making and design, I want to convey a thoughtfulness and empathy for the new art and design students—those who may have not had the same access as their peers, but who have the desire to create, learn, and create again and again.

One of my favorite professors at Rutgers, Peter Stroud used to ask us, "Did you choose *Art* or did *Art* choose you?" When asked, "How many of you have to make things?" all my students' hands go up. Why? What is the impulse to make things? I don't want to speculate on what is behind the drive to make things, and I'm not going to try to answer that question here—it is better taken up late at night in dark, crowded, noisy places. But I will tell you it is essential to a designer or artist. The drive to make, remake, experiment, try, fail, and get back to the work is an essential quality of all designers and artists. I cannot emphasize enough the fearless pursuit of the image, object, product, building, construction, interaction, video, performance, or whatever. We cannot move forward without experimentation, and we can't experiment with a fear of failure. Make it and we'll see if it works!

"Just in case" or "just in time." Books tend to fall into the category of "just in case"—giving you solutions to potential problems, just in case you encounter them. (If you encounter problem *A*, then see solution *B*.) Or, books especially dealing with software give you tasks, and then tell you how to solve them step by step, which still attempts to teach you something you might need just in case you find a situation like the task. This is a great way for some people to learn how to use the tool. But I have tried to write this book with a "just in time" outlook toward the building blocks of technique and understanding, in the hope of a larger understanding of the mindset needed to succeed in using the basic tools of digital media. To this end, I do not give any assignments—that I leave up to the faculty teaching you. But I give you the picture in broad strokes, with a constant emphasis on *intellectual curiosity*. I cannot hope to put all the information in a book that you can gather from Internet searching, asking an instructor, or asking a peer. I see this book as a push to get you started, but where you go is up to you, and your curiosity.

A BOOK IN TWO PARTS

I see this essential guide in two parts: one, the nuts and bolts of navigating the realms of digital imaging software; and two, the basics of design for designers and artists. I try to break down the software into their most fundamental parts, and give you just enough information so you can begin to explore the applications yourself. Also, with the basic design, I want to give you what you need to know, but not much more so you have room to experiment, and instructors have room to improvise, and riff on the material, and bring their own methodology to the classroom experience.

PART 1

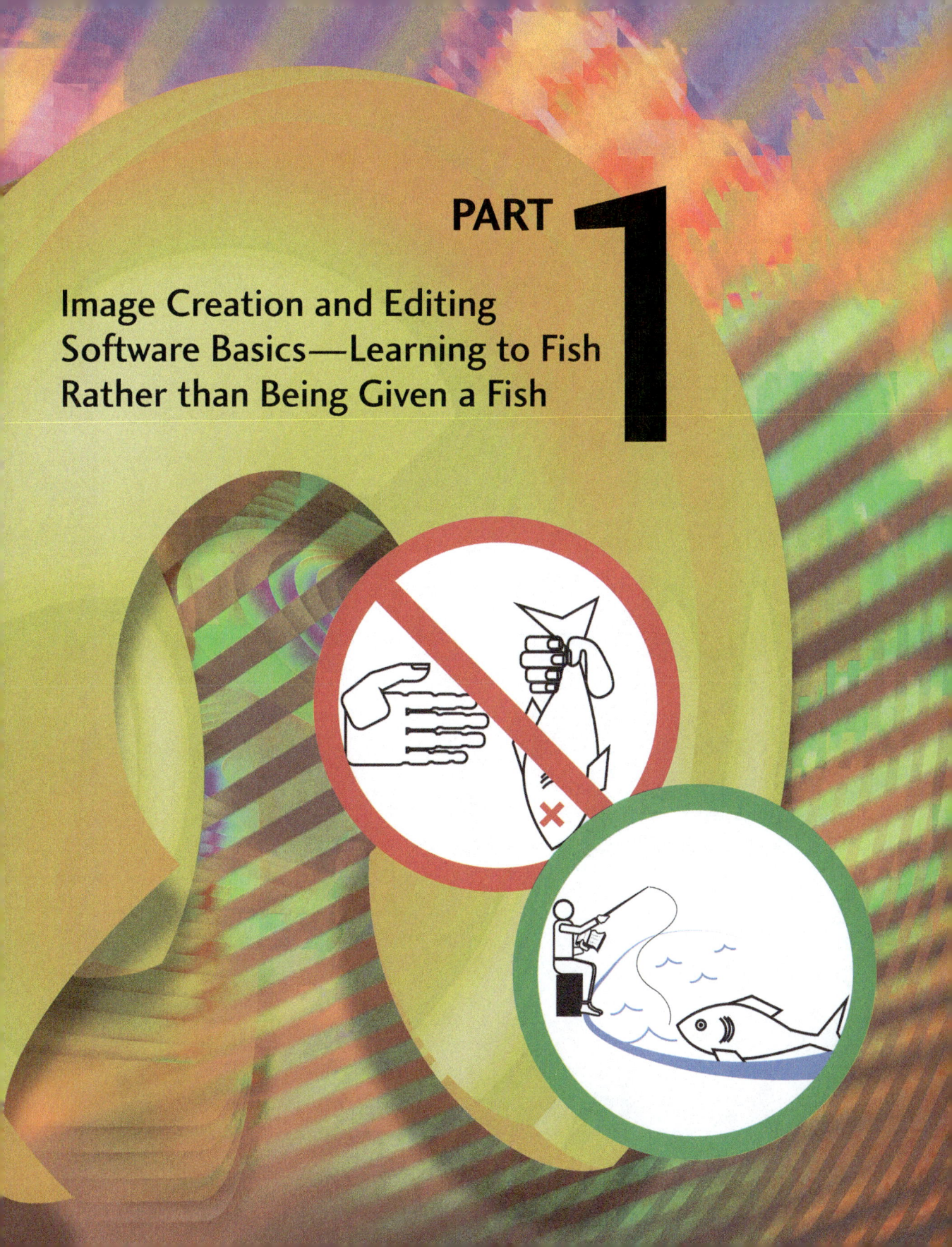

Image Creation and Editing Software Basics—Learning to Fish Rather than Being Given a Fish

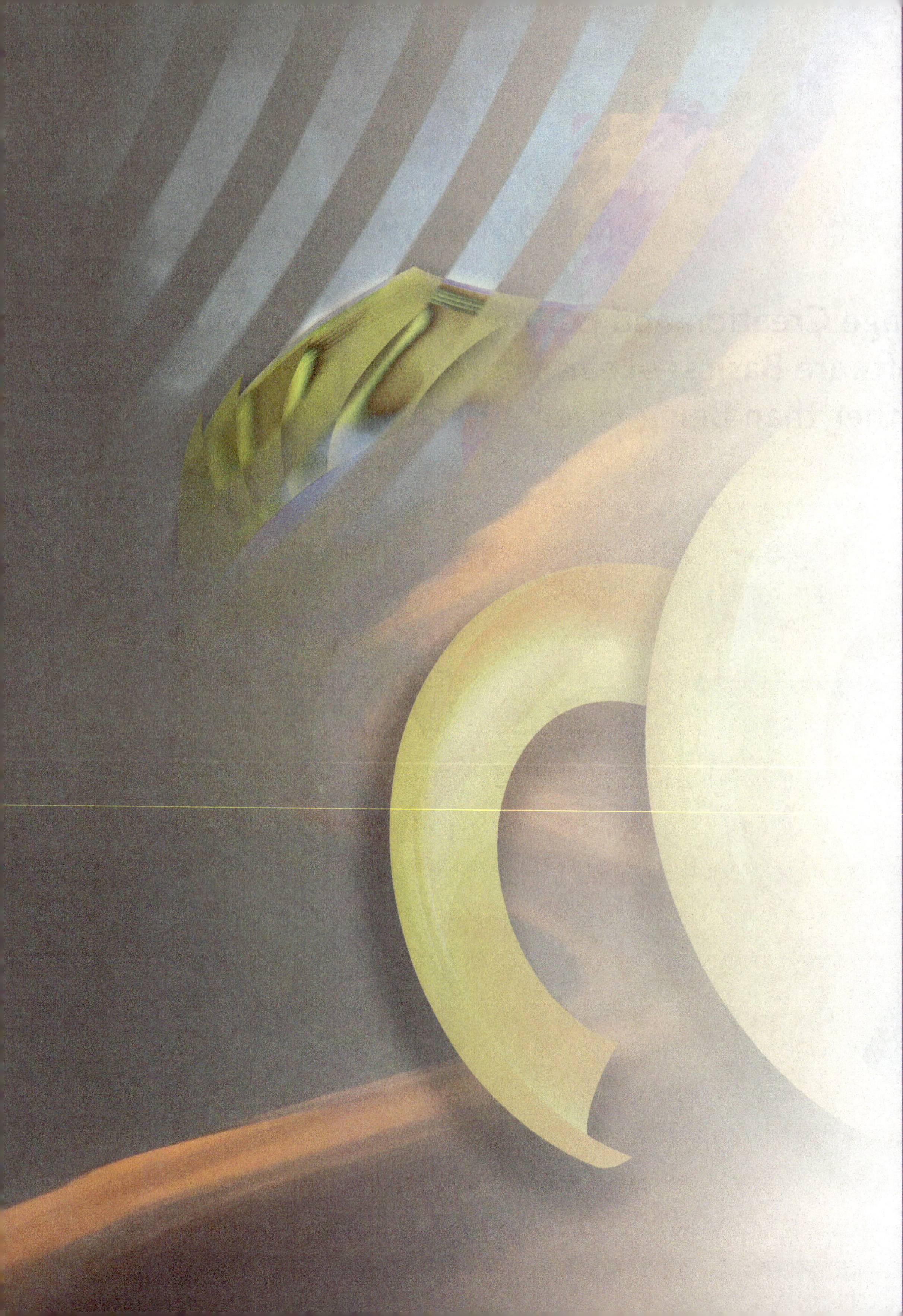

What Is Digital Media?

What is digital media? Basically, digital media is a set of programmed languages (built out of digits 1s and 0s; see explanation on binary[1]), which can be translated by a computer into an array of varying information. By computer, I am speaking about any device with computational processing abilities—that is, smartphones to microwave ovens. This information can include anything from a simple text file, to the instructions for 3D objects to be printed in real space at almost any scale, to ubiquitous digital video and audio. We are surrounded by digital media and interact with it in numerous forms on a daily basis (e.g., the Internet). I am going to focus on the applications of the Adobe Creative Cloud. Specifically, Adobe Photoshop, Illustrator, and InDesign. I will talk about and briefly cover HTML and CSS, as a very basic introduction to Web design and writing code for digital media interface design, and user experience design. I will also briefly talk about video editing and audio editing as they relate to digital media.

Ultimately, I will connect digital media to the basics of design essential to the art or design student as they explore the creation of projects and work through visual, contextual, practical, and philosophical problems in the building of a body of work in design or art.

---

1. A binary code represents text, computer processor instructions, or other data using any two-symbol system, but often the binary number system's 0 and 1. The binary code assigns a pattern of binary digits (bits) to each character, instruction, etc. For example, a binary string of 8 bits can represent any of 256 possible values and can therefore represent a variety of different items (Wikipedia).

ANALOG VERSUS DIGITAL

What is an analog? When we speak about analog media, we are speaking about a continuous uncoded relationship between the real thing and its representation. This relationship can be mechanical, as with an analog watch, or electrical as with an analog radio signal, or a combination, as in a vinyl record player, where the physical grooves in the record are directly translated into mechanical sound waves and electrically amplified. The defining feature of analog media is a direct relationship between the subject and the representation of it. If we think of an analog clock as a representation of time, we might also see it as an analog to the rotation of the earth, and that as an analog to how we experience time. I bring the analog into this discussion only because, although the environments in computer interface space are digital, our interactions with them in the design of graphical user interfaces (GUIs)[2] rely heavily on analogs of physical objects to hold meaning and utility for the user. Consider this example: The file system in a computer is an analog of a physical filing cabinet, with the drive acting as the cabinet filled with folders, in turn filled with files. This may seem like an intuitive step, which speaks more to the elegance of its design than to obvious understandability. Think for a moment about another system of creating and storing documents like *scrolls*. How would our computer interfaces look and function if we had used

---

2. GUI (graphical user interface) was first developed and used by Xerox PARC (Palo Alto Research Center Incorporated) in 1973. Later the Apple Macintosh 128K in 1984, and Atari ST and Commodore Amiga in 1985, all using GUIs. Search GUI for more information.

Introduction to Digital Media for Designers and Artists

scrolls instead of *files*? We might have *rooms* or *racks* instead of *folders*, and all documents might have to be understood in terms of *lines* instead of *pages* (because a scroll is continuous)!

This brings us to a discussion of metaphor. What is a metaphor? From high school English class we understand a metaphor to be the use of a literal meaning for another meaning in order to compare, emphasize, or illuminate (e.g., "right now I am swimming in work to do"). If we think about art and design as visual language, metaphor and metonymy[3] become very important in both communicating your idea with power and understanding the things you make—as well as the things you see. This process of creating images and understanding images requires a deep and liberal understanding of culture, and the products of culture, from soapbox design to video games and movies. The more you see, read, and experience the better positioned you are as a designer or artist to create comprehensible work at its most basic; and elegant, clever, funny, and brilliant work at its best. The power of the computer as a tool for art and design cannot make up for experience, practice, and immersion in the culture of your chosen field.

SEARCH TERMS

Analog, Analogy, Apple Computer History, GUI, Media, Metaphor, Metonymy, Microsoft History, Operating System, Semiotics, Xerox PARC

THE COMPUTER AS A TOOL

We need to think about the computer as an art and design tool, like a pencil, paint brush, Xacto knife, etc. As with the use of any tool the more you practice with it the better you become. My wish for you is for the computer to become a natural extension of you in your creative process. With this said, I want to give you some basic insight into the quick workings of common art and design software. This book is focused on the Adobe Creative Cloud suite of software, and specifically the 2D aspects of Photoshop, Illustrator, and InDesign. But, the information I am going to discuss here will have uses across many other applications. I want to unpack—just a little bit—the graphical user interface (GUI), and specifically the user interfaces (UIs), common to almost every image, video and sound creation, and editing software application in the world today.

With regard to what kind of computer you will be working on, and which operating system, there are two choices (excluding working in other environments and on other devices, where you may also have image editing software), Mac OS or Windows. As far as I am concerned it does not matter to me, as I don't take sides in the debate. The only thing I care about is the differences, and a couple I will note here.

---

3. Metonymy is a figure of speech that consists of the use of the name of one object or concept for that of another to which it is related, or of which it is a part. For example, "The orders came for Albany" indicates Albany is a metonym for the capitol of New York state.

Mac OS	Windows
command + key	control + key
Command + click = right click	

For our use as we progress the main difference is going to be *command* + for Mac OS and *control* + for Windows. With regard to function keys (F1, F2, etc.) different computer manufacturers arrange these keys and how to activate them differently, but generally there is an *fn* key. I would urge you to get to know your machine, and get used to its quirks and ticks. The tools we use help to create the things we need to make, and in turn we tend to personalize the look and feel of the tool. As much as I would encourage customizing *your* computer, I would conversely urge you *not* to customize the work environments of classroom computers and communal labs. Being conscientious as a designer or artist will serve you well as you progress.

INTELLECTUAL CURIOSITY

I cannot do this on my own. I need you, the reader, to have an open mind and a keen intellectual curiosity about all things, but specifically the inner workings of software. I want you to feel a freedom to explore the applications with wide-eyed excitement. I am acting as a coach and motivational speaker so *you* can fearlessly find what you love about the software and what it can do for you as a designer or artist. Don't be afraid to fail—I will show you the reset button! And don't be afraid to ask questions of your instructors, your friends, and the Internet. As these applications have progressed over the years, features have been built on features, some things have been brought to the fore while others have been hidden within menus; always there are new features. The new versions of these applications come out with more and more frequent regularity, sometimes with substantial changes and additions. I will give you the basic basics, but you will need to be sharp and constantly aware of the *new* if you wish to travel down this road.

Camille Corot, *The Curious Little Girl*

Courtesy of The Metropolitan Museum of Art, and The Walter H. and Leonore Annenberg Collection, Gift of Walter H. and Leonore Annenberg, 1999, Bequest of Walter H. Annenberg, 2002.

Introduction to Digital Media for Designers and Artists

Application Basics

MAC OS KEY FEATURES

With the price of personal computers dropping all the time, and our access to them in school, at the library, at play, and at work being nearly universal in the United States and the industrialized world, I am going to make the grand assertion most of you reading this know how to navigate a computer. I am going to assume this computer is a Microsoft Windows–based machine. I am also going to assume, even if your school is Windows based, you will as a designer or artist encounter an Apple Mac OS–based environment. As designers love to point out, most things you see as graphic design were designed on a Mac—even logos for rival operating systems.

The *Apple* menu, in the upper left corner of the screen, tells you about the computer, sets the preferences, and sleeps, restarts, or shuts down the computer.

The *Finder* in the bottom left of the *Dock* (usually, although it can be moved) is where one gains access to the Mac OS filing system. You can open up multiple Finder windows, and files can be dragged from place to place. Holding down the *Alt (option)* key will copy the file being dragged instead of moving the file if one is operating in the same drive. Files are always copied if dragged from one drive to another drive.

Left Click, Right Click

The left click on a mouse is the standard click. The right click usually brings up more options on whatever you are clicking. Note that on older Macs with only one button, a right click is accomplished by holding *control + click*.

DISCLOSURE TRIANGLES, HAMBURGER MENUS, AND TIMELESS TOOLS

Definition: *Anachronism*—an object, people, or situations out of a correct chronological or historical time.

Much of what we deal with in menu design, placement, and use are adapted from other times. For example, word processing applications, by their nature, fall back onto tropes employed by typewriters, even as most of the people reading this book right now have never used a typewriter. Another example is the pen tool. The pen tool in almost any Adobe application looks like a fountain pen, which was invented in 1827; and I would venture to guess most readers also have not used this type of pen. My point or assumption is we understand these anachronistic images because of a perceived common culture. My intuition and experience tell me I need to stress the point of research, context clues, and further education into the history of pretty much everything, because these tools are *not* always obvious and can present a challenge for the novice, less privileged, or oblivious student. The scope of basic graphic interface clues can be vast, but I want to focus specifically on those employed most by Adobe in three main applications: Photoshop, Illustrator, and InDesign.

The first is the disclosure triangle (or sometimes called a disclosure widget).

This little black, white, or grey triangle in the corner of menus simply means there is more information on or *under* this object and one needs to *click* on it to find what is underneath. There is usually a logic to the disclosure. Similar tools or expanded menus tend to be grouped *under* the disclosure triangle. I urge you to be curious and discover this for yourself.

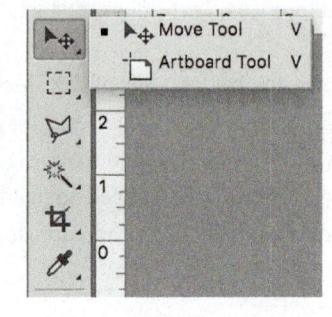

Introduction to Digital Media for Designers and Artists

The second of our graphical menus is the hamburger menu (also called the hamburger button, options button, menu button, or even the pancake or hotdog button). These buttons simply look like a stack of lines. A hamburger menu indicates there is more information to be had by clicking on the button.

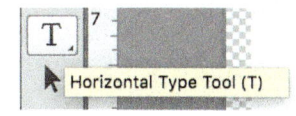

Another tip is to just leave your mouse over a tool in an Adobe application, and most of the time it will bring up a yellow box with the name of the tool with the keyboard shortcut to the tool.

UNDERSTANDING CONTEXT AND VISUAL CUES

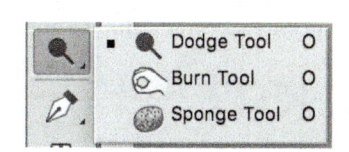

As a note on interface design anachronism: In Adobe Photoshop, the Burn and Dodge tools are a nod to wet darkroom photography—a practice most contemporary design students have very little experience in. The symbols themselves reference tools used to block out the light from a photographic enlarger. The Dodge tool resembles a piece of cardstock on the end of a rod to selectively block out the light from the photographic paper; the Burn tool resembles a hand with the shape of an "O" to selectively add more light onto an area of the photographic paper. The more obvious anachronistic sign is the "telephone" symbol on mobile phone interfaces.

Keyboard Shortcut Keys

What is a shortcut key? A shortcut key is a keyboard key or combination of keys that replace having to manually move the mouse to click on a menu item. For example (in most software), one can go up to *edit* and find *copy* or *paste*, and after selecting an object one can move the mouse up to *edit*, select *copy*, move the mouse to another space in the file, *click* to affix the cursor or select the layer, move the mouse back up to *edit*, and select *paste* to paste the object in the new place. This is a lot of moving the mouse around. Keyboard shortcuts allow us the stay focused in the workspace without having to move the mouse up to the menu constantly; they also allow us to perform repetitive tasks with great speed.
Adobe Software in general:

CHAPTER 2: **Application Basics**

	Windows	Mac OS
Undo	Ctrl + Z (Photoshop: Ctrl+Z toggles 1-step undo/redo, to multiple undo, Alt+Ctrl+Z)	Command + Z (Photoshop: Command+Z toggles 1-step undo/redo, to multiple undo, Option+Command+Z)
Redo	Shift + Ctrl + Z	Shift + Command + Z
Cut	Ctrl + X	Command + X
Copy	Ctrl + C	Command + C
Paste	Ctrl + V	Command + V

Specific keys for Adobe Photoshop: Command + d = deselect

NOTE

Command + d (control + d in Windows) in Photoshop is extremely important. If at any time in Photoshop none of your tools seem to be working it could be because you have a very small selection somewhere on the image. Most tools will only work inside the selected area. By de-selecting you remove the selection and free Photoshop to work in your desired location on the image.

Specific keys for Adobe Illustrator:
Command + d = repeat last instruction
Specific keys for Adobe InDesign:
Option (alt) + Shift + Command + n = insert current page number

NOTE

When using this in Master Pages a letter code will be inserted corresponding to the letter of the Master Page.

SEARCH TERMS

Adobe Application Shortcut Keys, Shortcut Keys

THE BASIC IDEAS OF DIGITAL MEDIA APPLICATIONS

Raster versus Vector

A key to understanding computer graphics is understanding the differences between raster graphics and vector graphics. Basically, raster graphics are described as images constructed out of a grid of pixels, and a pixel can best be described as a very small square or dot of color.

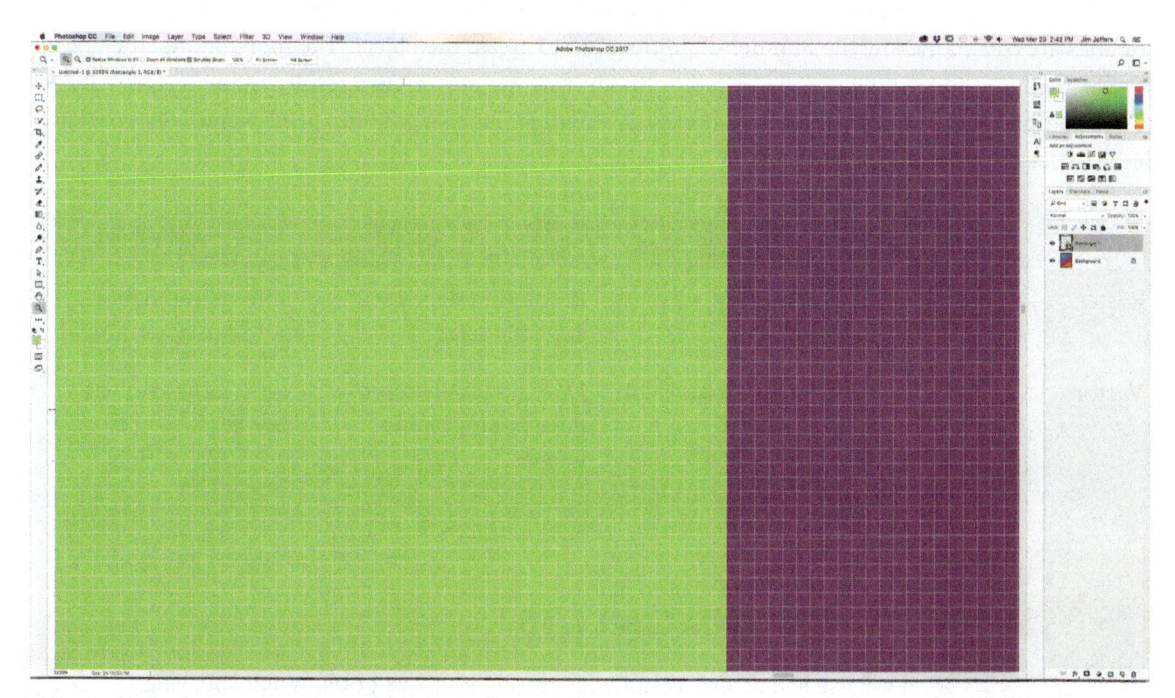

Closeup of a raster image at 3200%

Vector images are basically objects that are constructed mathematically. They are made out of points, attached by lines, and given curve control by what is known as Bézier curves.

Vector graphic showing Bézier curves with handles

CHAPTER 2: **Application Basics**

Each type of graphic has its specialty. Raster graphics are good at simulating continuous color as in photographs and are therefore the graphic type we use when doing photo manipulation. The limitation of raster graphics comes when we try to enlarge them, because they are resolution dependent. This means the number of original pixels in an image is fixed at the start of the image's creation, which also explains why we make such a big deal about the megapixels of a camera. The only way a raster image can get bigger is by adding more pixels by a process called interpolation. This process necessarily affects the image's quality, as the computer is pulling original pixels apart and using sophisticated algorithms to fill in the pixels in between. Vector graphics are not constrained by resolution, as mathematical constructions, they can be enlarged or reduced without losing quality. However, as mathematical constructions, vector graphics are constrained by the number of points used to create the object. The more points, the bigger the file, the more computing power needed to manipulate the object. As a result, vector images tend to be less complex, but this is excellent for a huge scope of digital media graphics needs: logos, text, package design, stickers, billboards, and the like.

Graphic Type	Pros	Cons	Best uses
Raster	Photographic quality images	Resolution dependent, large file sizes	Photo manipulation, photo-based graphics
Vector	Resolution independent	Does not easily reproduce photographic images	Logos, large areas of color, text

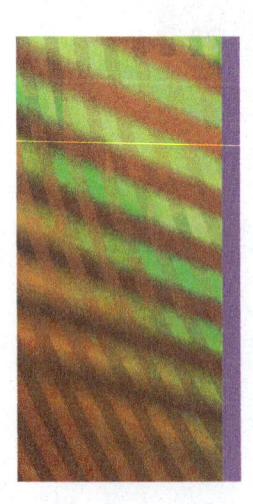

IMAGES AND OBJECTS

I will use image and object a lot throughout this book. When speaking of an image, I will generally be referring to a group of pixels in the form of a photograph or photographic-related image, or a rasterized object (an object turned into pixels). When I am referring to an object, this is me leaving the door open to the most possibilities of visual elements. An object could be text, a circle, a 3D form, a logo, and so forth. Generally, objects will have variable properties (e.g., the size of a stroke around a circle, the fill, the font).

I need to also mention text. Text is, as you might have intuited, a special kind of object. While text is rendered as vectors, it is edited as text. Text has a few positional attributes (which I will discuss in depth). For our purpose here, editable text—meaning text that has not been rasterized or turned into outlines—requires the font to be installed on the machine where you are attempting to edit. This is very important when moving files from machine to machine that you are aware of this.

The Layer

Layers allow the user to put one image or object "on top" of another. In the process, certain aspects of the layer can be manipulated to a variety of effects. The most basic are position and opacity. Layers give you control of where another image is positioned not only in *x-y* space (up, down, left, right) but also *z* space (in front, behind).

Layers give us control of opacity, or how "see-through" an image or object is. They also allow the user to direct only certain effects to one layer and leave the others unaffected. With this said, layers can also affect the underlying layers depending on use. The layer is a super powerful invention, and is partly responsible for the way graphics are created today. We need only look at package design, advertising, and contemporary fine art to see layers at work.

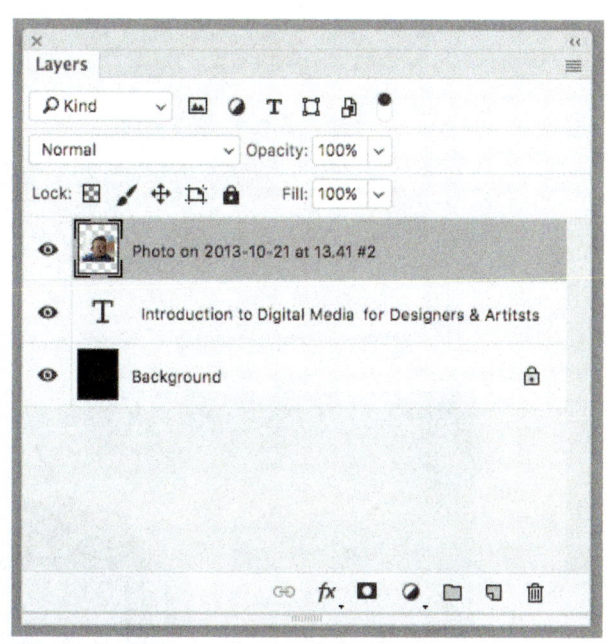

Photoshop layer menu

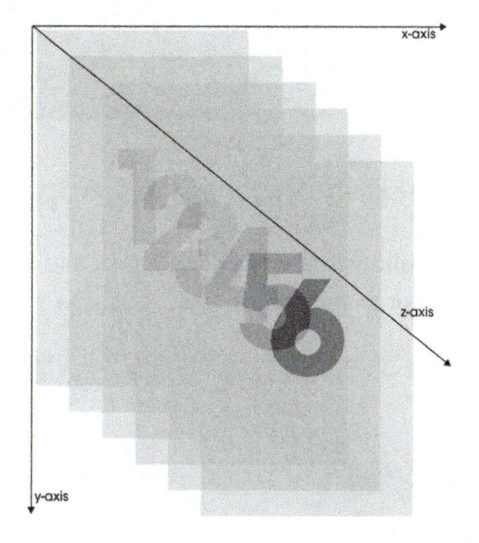

CHAPTER 2: Application Basics

Selection Tools across Applications

Photoshop: These Marquee, Lasso, and Selection tools allow the user to select any part of an image, based on numerous criteria (e.g., shape, color, edge contrast).

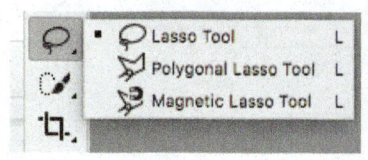

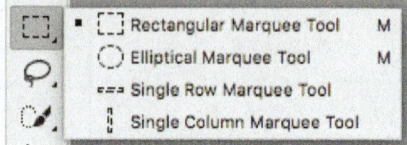

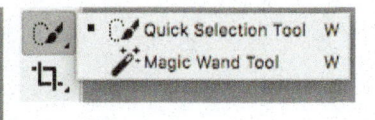

14

Introduction to Digital Media for Designers and Artists

Illustrator: These selection tools are common to vector-based editing in the Adobe suite. They allow you to select the whole object, just one point, or part of a grouped object. The Magic Wand tool works similar to Photoshop, as it selects objects based on consistent color of a user-determined piece of the object.

In Adobe InDesign, the selection tools function nearly identical to Illustrator.

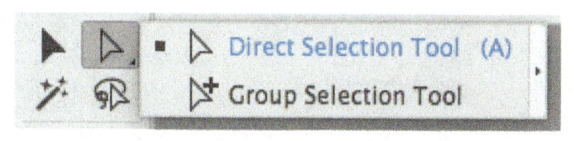

> **NOTE**
>
> Most of these tools have properties that can be changed as needed. These can either be found on the property bar or by double-clicking on the tool.

Copying, Cloning, and Content Aware

Being able to *copy* and *paste* images, parts of images, objects, and parts of objects from one place to another and from one layer to another is a basic function of Adobe's Photoshop and Illustrator. Most of us understand the basic idea of *copy-paste* from using word processing software, Internet browsers, and even smartphones. The basic concept in Photoshop, Illustrator, and InDesign is the same; however, with the added power of layers, these applications add a third dimension to the idea—that is, we can put objects and images "on top of" not just "next to" another. Photoshop takes this power further with the idea of *cloning,* where the user can "paint" the image from one location to another, thus truly getting to the power of photo manipulation.

Using Photoshop's Clone Stamp tool one can copy from one area of the image to another. The tool works by deciding on the area to be cloned from, and holding down the *Option (Alt) key + clicking.*

Introduction to Digital Media for Designers and Artists

Notice I cloned into another layer. This way the original is unaltered and can be resampled if needed. I can also reposition the top layer as needed.

CHAPTER 2: Application Basics

With later versions of Photoshop, Adobe has included a Content Aware feature, which takes samples from the surrounding area and with great sophistication fills in the selection.

Introduction to Digital Media for Designers and Artists

As you can see from the example, Content Aware is not perfect but it can be a first move toward erasing something from an image. To use this feature, one makes a selection, then right-clicks on the selection to find the list with "fill…" and from here the Content Aware can be engaged.

> **NOTE**
>
> Most digital imaging software is context sensitive when *right-clicking*—for example, *right-clicking* over a selection is different from *right-clicking* on a menu.

CHAPTER 2: Application Basics

Masking

Masking is one of the most important concepts to understand and bring to bare on your projects as a digital media user. A mask lets you block out or *mask* parts of images allowing background information to show through. You can do this without erasing or damaging the *masked* image. Why is this important? Imagine you are working for a busy magazine and you just spent 45 minutes carefully erasing the background of a photo. In the background was a bunch of flowers. Your art director comes up to you and then looks at the masterful job you did erasing the background, and says, "Good job, but let's try it with the flowers." Because you erased the background you are going to have to find the original image and get the flowers back. However, if you had used a mask, you would simply remove the mask from the area of the flowers, and there you go. The difference is time, and time is what we are all trying to save.

ADOBE PHOTOSHOP

Step 1

Introduction to Digital Media for Designers and Artists

Step 2

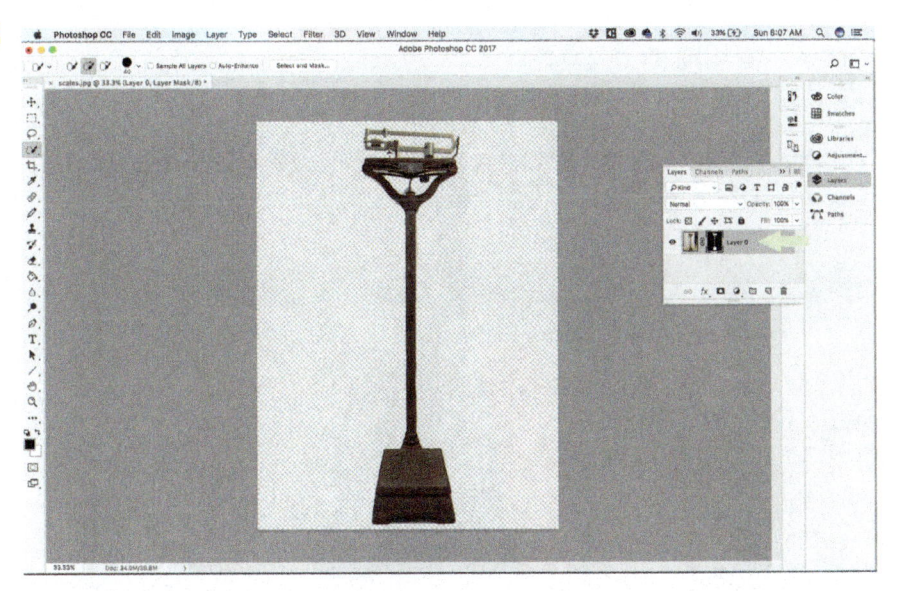

Step 3

CHAPTER 2: Application Basics

ADOBE ILLUSTRATOR

Step 1

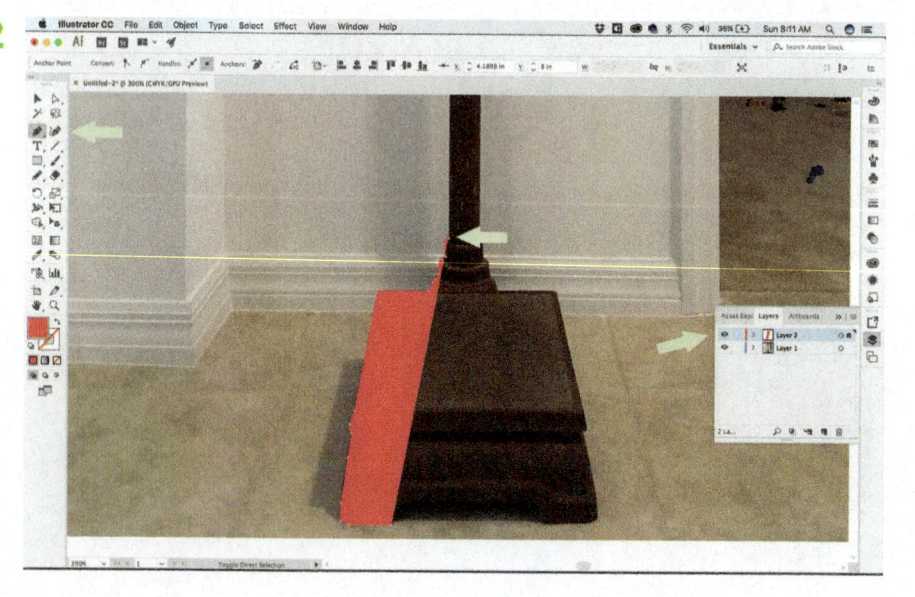

Step 2

Introduction to Digital Media for Designers and Artists

Step 3

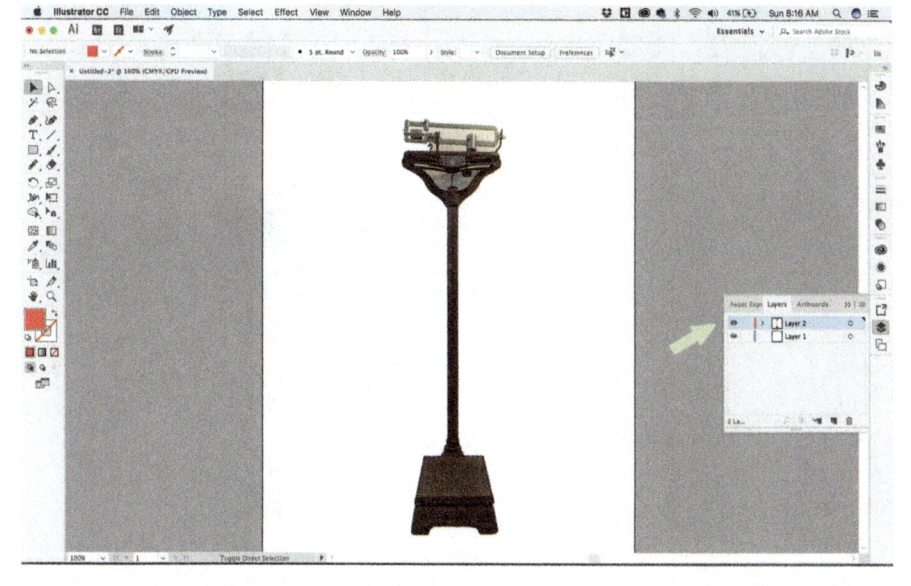

Step 4

CHAPTER 2: Application Basics

ADOBE INDESIGN

Step 1

Step 2

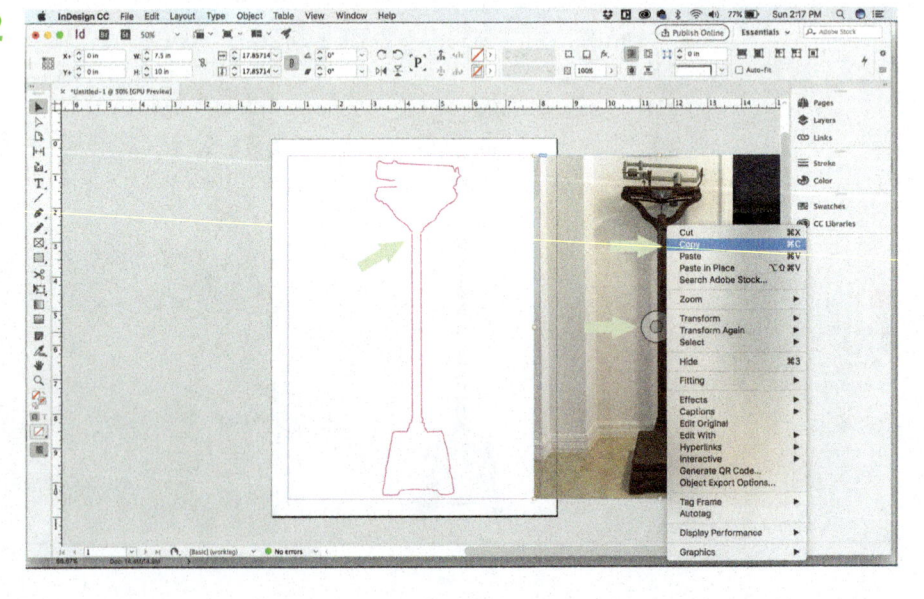

Introduction to Digital Media for Designers and Artists

Step 3

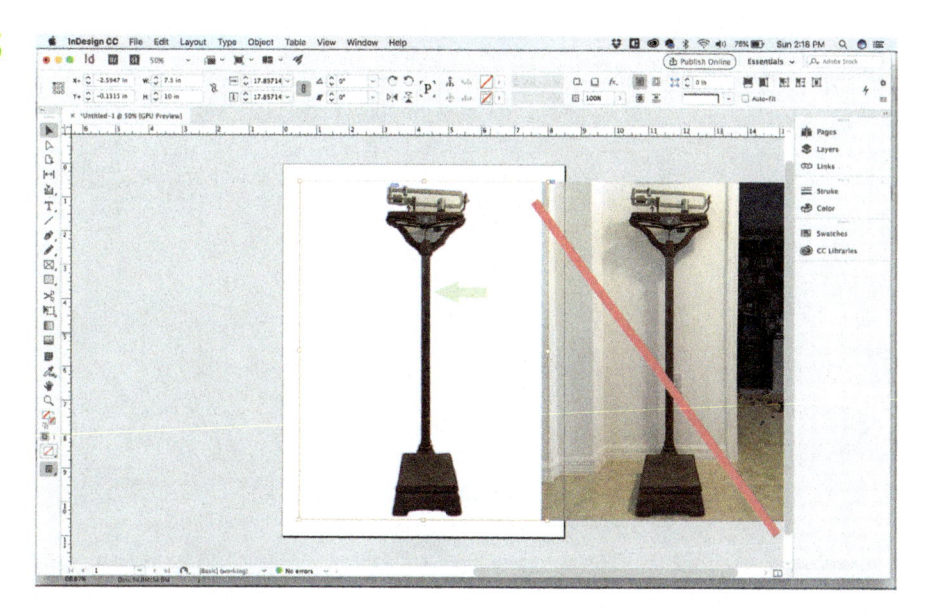

Step 4

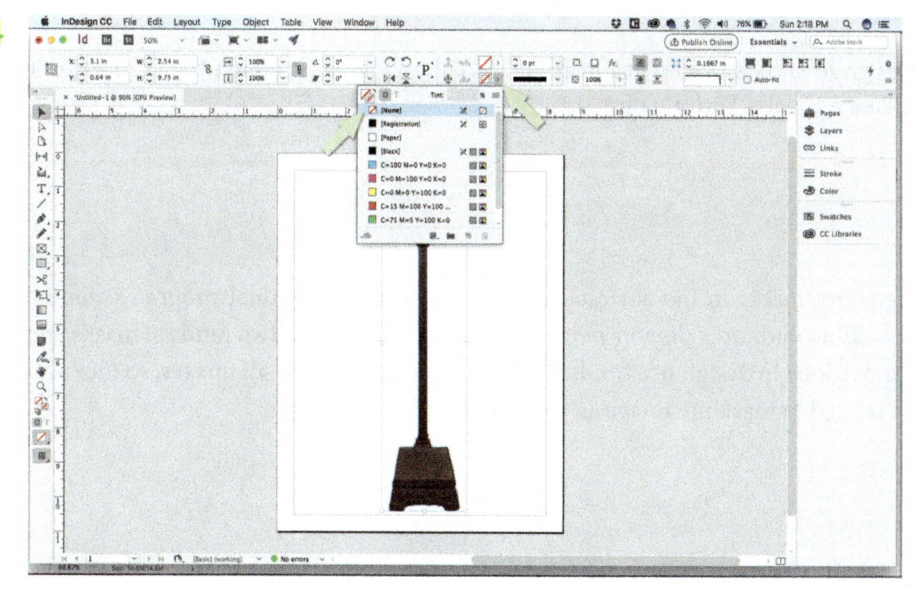

CHAPTER 2: Application Basics

25

Step 5

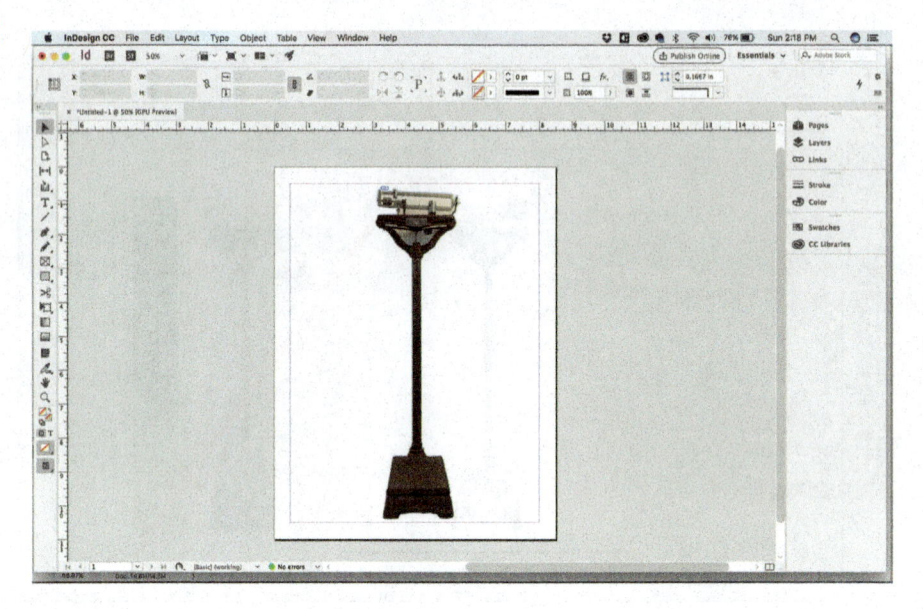

> ## NOTE
>
> For InDesign to show a placed image at full resolution you must adjust the Display Performance. View > Display Performance

I am talking about masks in the abstract. As we go into the individual programs some of the terms change. Adobe Illustrator uses *clipping masks*. Adobe Photoshop uses two kinds of masks, *masks* and *vector masks*. And Adobe InDesign uses *frames*, which are always around all images, so they are not applied, they are just resized to mask the image as you see fit.

Color in Digital Media (a First Look)

Artists and designers work with color. We live in a colorful world. I am going to briefly speak about color here, as I will go into much greater depths in the design section of this book.

You will need to know two things about color just to get you started with the Adobe applications: RGB and CMYK. These are the primary colors in the two modes color artists and designers deal with the most: screen and print.

RGB stands for red, green, and blue. These are the primary colors of projected light or additive color. This is the color used by your monitor, television, smartphone, tablet, video projector, among others.

Additive Color, RGB					**Subtractive Color, CMYK**

NOTE

RGB color is needed for files to be fully editable in Photoshop. If you ever find some of your filters greyed out, check your *color mode*.

CHAPTER 2: Application Basics

CMYK stands for cyan, magenta, yellow, and black. These are the primary colors for print, also referred to as process color or subtractive color. These colors correspond to the primary colors one learns when mixing pigmented color: blue, red, and yellow.

For our brief mention of color here, just know a couple of things: RGB files are for projected projects, like websites. CMYK files are for your print projects.

I need to also mention a couple of other color modes:

Color Mode	Use
Bitmap	Only black and white, greys are accomplished with halftones or dithers
Grayscale	Only shades of gray
Duotone	Duotone, two-color images; tritone, three-color images; quadtone, four-color images Individual colors can be specified
Indexed Color	Image where every color is specified in order to save file size; generally these files are used for the Web with .png or .gif extensions
RGB Color	Red, green, blue used in Photoshop to get the most editing tools available; RGB files are used for onscreen or projected graphics
CMYK Color	Cyan, magenta, yellow, and black used to simulate printed color; CMYK files are used for print
Lab Color	A color space designed to come very close to the number of colors perceived by the human eye; can be used to make very precise color corrections
Multichannel Images	Images that contain 256 levels of gray in each channel; used for specialized printing where multiple colors are specified

NOTE

Color channels are the grayscale images for each color in a particular mode. For example, a CMYK image would have four color channels. In Photoshop, masks also show up as channels. Channels can be used to make specific selections. And in printing, channels can be used for a specified color.

In the world of printing we have specified color, and color systems like Pantone, where a set of managed colors can be specified from a book, on a particular stock of paper, to ensure a color match.

Color for the Web is another matter, and I will cover it in depth in the design section. As a brief summation, color for the Web is specified in a few ways: Names, Internet browsers can read simple color names (red, blue, green, black, white, pink, etc.). Hexadecimal color involves three two-digit values ranging from A–F and 0–9, with the three sets representing R, G, and B values (e.g., #FF0000 = red, #00FF00 = green, #0000FF = blue, #000000 = black, #FFFFFF = white, #FFC0CB = pink). Contemporary Web browsers also understand a few other color spaces, rgb, rgba, where *a* is for alpha (transparency). These are written like this: rgb(255,0,0), with the color amount of each channel ranging from 0–255, and rgba(0,255,0,0.5), with the alpha ranging from 0.0 (fully transparent) to 1.0 (opaque).

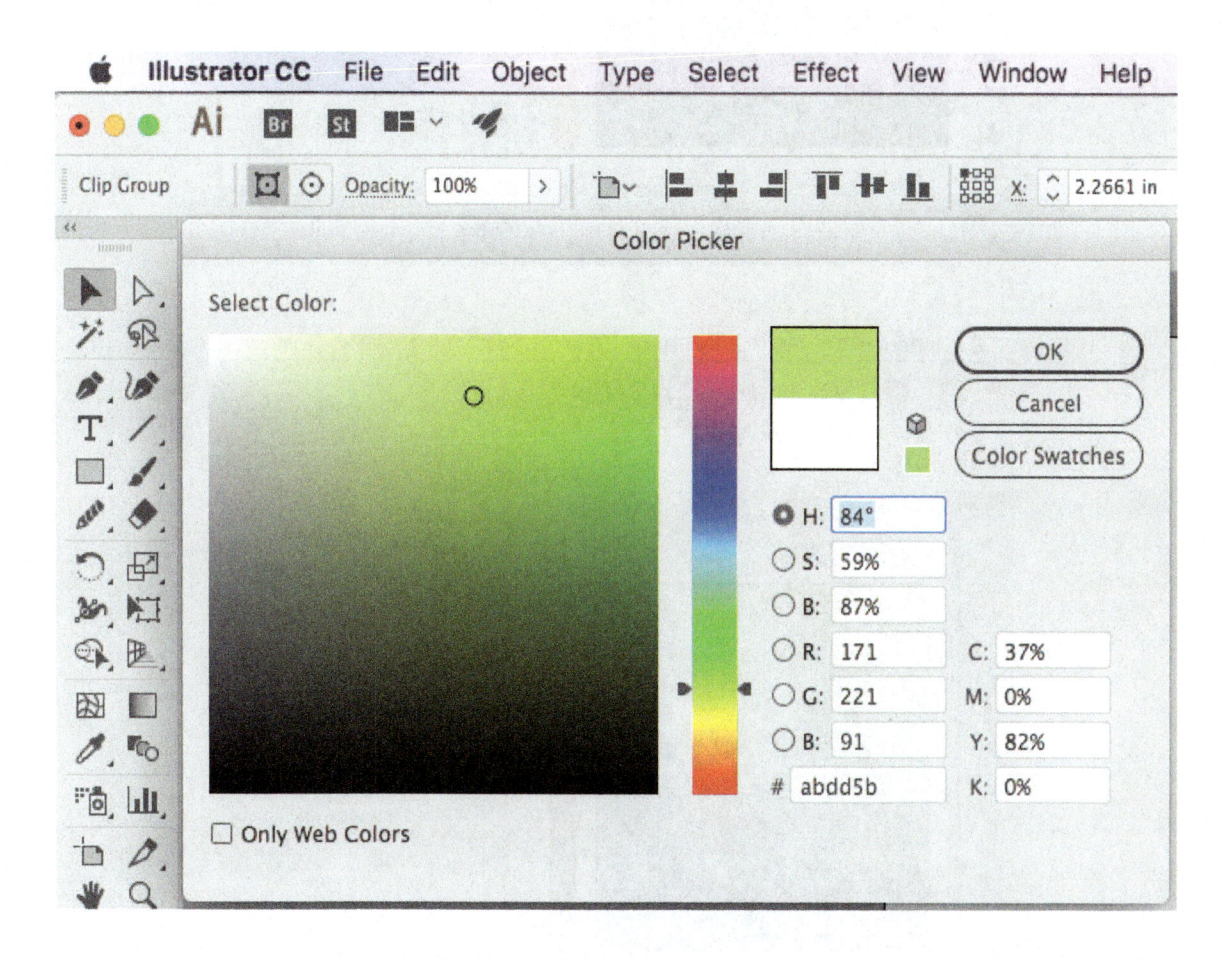

CHAPTER 2: **Application Basics**

29

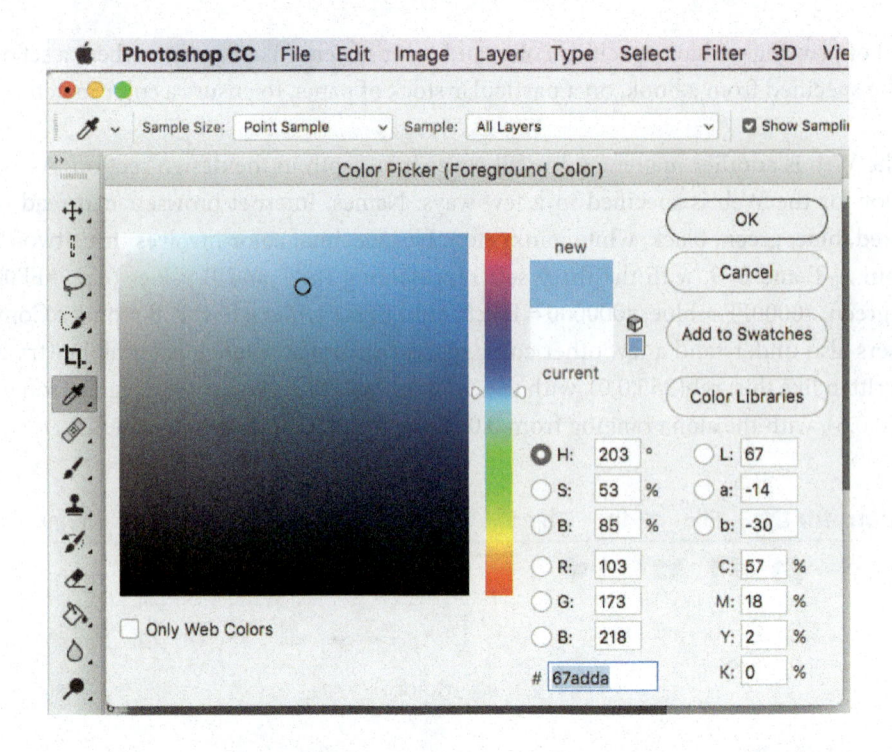

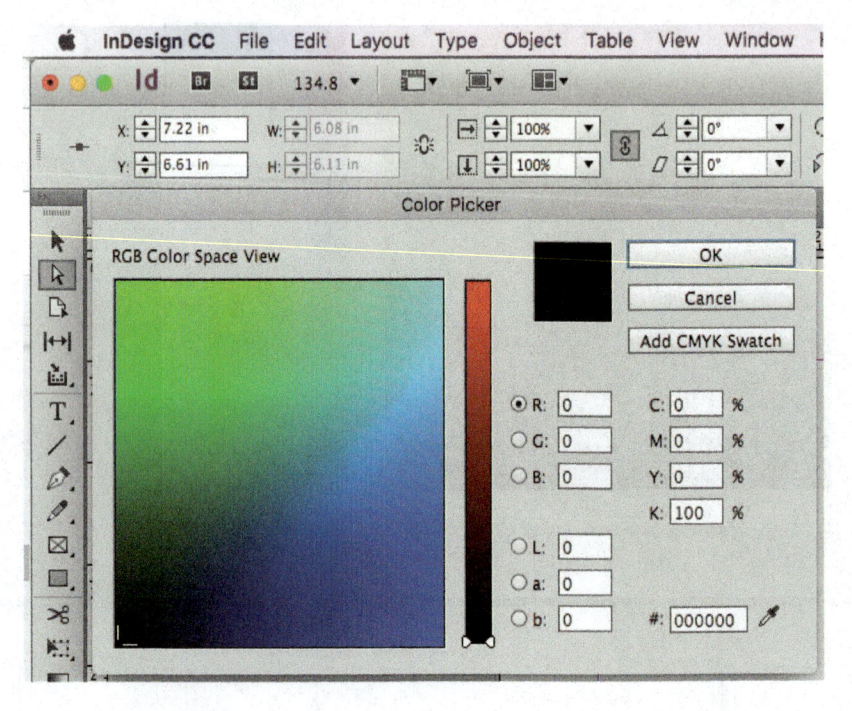

30   **Introduction to Digital Media for Designers and Artists**

Cascading Information: Centrally Located and Distributed to Multiple Elements

Master Pages in InDesign, and CSS in Web Design

The idea of centralized information is a very important concept to understand and internalize in order to gain a rich understanding of digital media. When we think of storing all the instructions in one place it makes sense, as we might do this physically in the general organization of any given set of information or objects. However, the next step in digital media is the idea that, if we change something in our cluster of instructions it travels throughout the system to change things on a grand scale. We might think of a radio station broadcasting from one central place to every radio tuned to the correct frequency.

In Adobe InDesign this distribution or cascading of information is accomplished through the idea of *Master Pages*. *Master Pages* set information that will be on every page in the document. Imagine a book, and in this book you want page numbers, consistent page graphics, chapter headings at the top of the page, etc. Now, imagine the book is 1,000 pages long. If you had to manually insert page numbers on every page, you would face an enormous amount of work. What *Master Pages* allows you to do is set up these consistent elements in one place, and have them affect *all* of the pages you desire.

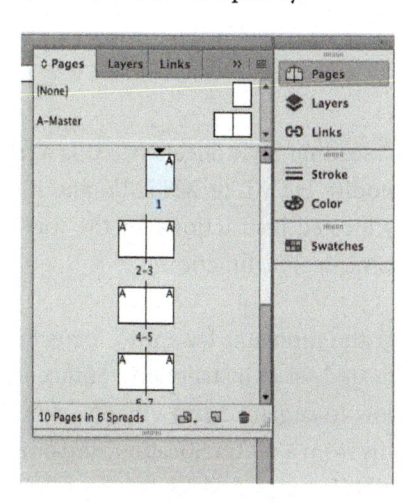

NOTE

Layer order is consistent between Master Pages and document pages, but content is not. You can only edit Master Page elements in Master Pages, and you do that by *double-clicking* on the Master Pages icon.

CHAPTER 2: Application Basics

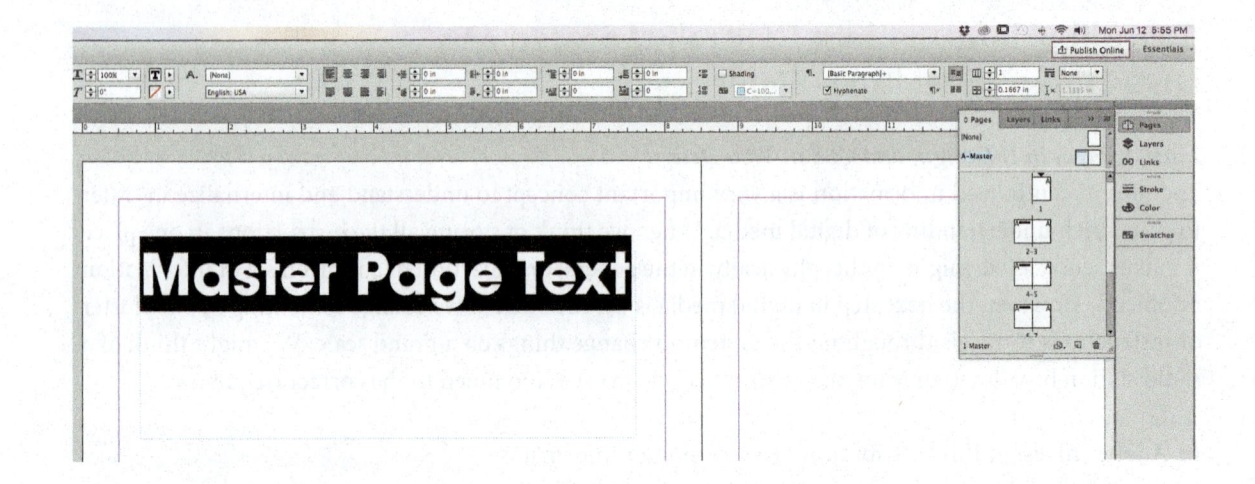

Cascading Style Sheets (CSS) is a markup language used to modify HTML or XHTML, and it can function as centrally located instructions for the way Web pages look and, to some degree, function.

At the moment, I want to focus on the idea of a centrally located set of instructions. Suffice it to say, CSS tells HTML how to organize and visually structure Web pages. It does this from a central location, and one CSS file can affect many HTML pages. It does this by sending instructions to named objects or elements. These can either be whole built-in elements of HTML or user-determined variables associated with either a unique or general selector within an element.

This is a fairly simple idea. Imagine a room filled with students, and you need to have them do something. You could address *students*, in which case ALL *students* would be activated, or you could address them by a *name*, and then you would only have a specific student do the action. See the example script.

> **NOTE**
>
> There will be a section of this book dedicated to giving you a basic understanding of how HTML and CSS work to create Web pages.

Introduction to Digital Media for Designers and Artists

```html
1    <html>
2    <head>
3    <style type="text/css">
4    body  {
5           background-color: black;
6    }
7    #centerHolder {
8           width: 300px;
9           height: 300px;
10          Margin: 0px auto;
11          background-color: white;
12   }
13   p {
14          color: red;
15   }
16   .textChange {
17          font-style: italic;
18   }
19   .textBold {
20          font-weight: bold;
21   }
22   </style>
23   </head>
24   <body>
25   
26   <div id="centerHolder">
27   
28   <p> Now is the time for <span class="textChange">all</span> great people to come to the aid of <span class="textChange textBold">visual culture</span>.
29   </p>
30   
31   </div>
32   
33   </body>
34   </html>
35   
36   
```

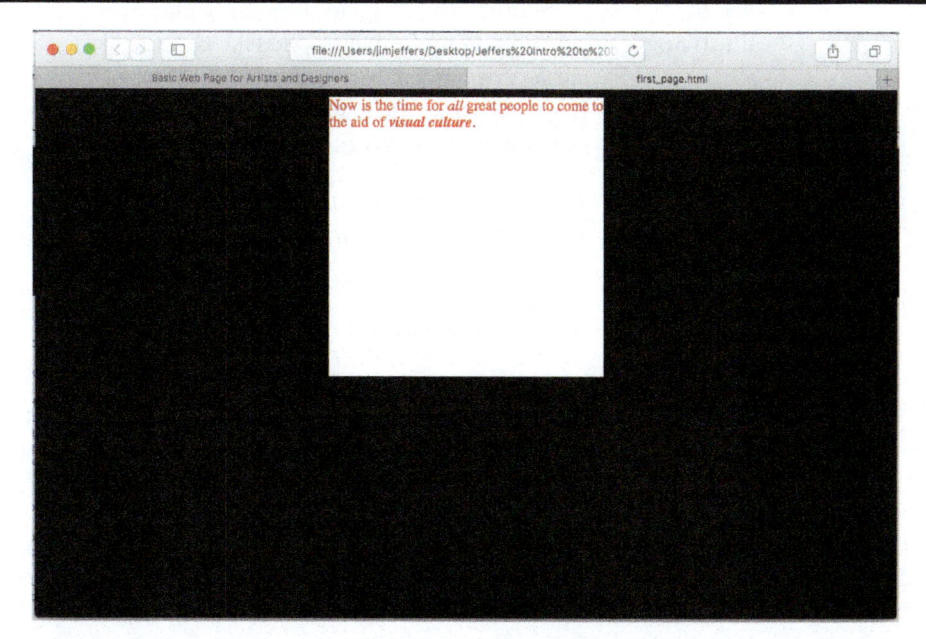

CHAPTER 2: Application Basics

This script if saved as an .html file, and then opened in a browser renders a black page, with a white centered box, with red text in it.

Common File Formats and Their Uses

Before I begin with a long list of file types, their uses, and programs, I want to talk about the (.) extension. The (.) extension tells you and the application what type of file you are trying to open, write, modify, etc. Personally, I find it hard when the operating system hides my file extensions. And as a Web designer this hiding feature should always be disabled; you need to know if it is an .html file or a .psd file. You are only seeing half the picture if your file extensions are hidden.

Some file formats are uncompressed and contain all the data, allowing the user to edit the file. Other file formats are compressed and designed for the proofing of documents or the publication of images, animations, or videos.

Some Useful Image File Formats

File Type (.extension)	Editing / Writing Program	Notes	Compressed
.ai	Adobe Illustrator	These are primarily vector files, but .ai files can contain raster information and text. Note: .ai files are very dependent on what version of Adobe Illustrator wrote them. Please check the version of AI, and you can *Save As* a legacy format.	
.psd	Adobe Photoshop	These are primarily raster files, but .psd files can contain raster information and text.	

File Type (.extension)	Editing / Writing Program	Notes	Compressed
.3fr, .ari, .arw, .bay, .crw, .cr2, .cap, .data, .dcs, .dcr, .dng, .drf, .eip, .erf, .fff, .gpr, .iiq, .k25, .kdc, .mdc, .mef, .mos, .mrw, .nef, .nrw, .obm, .orf, .pef, .ptx, .pxn, .r3d, .raf, .raw, .rwl, .rw2, .rwz, .sr2, .srf, .srw, .tif, .x3f	Adobe Photoshop / Raw photo formats created by digital camera, or created from other digital camera files	These are raster files containing all the data created when taking a digital photograph on a raw-capable camera. These files have a lot more data than a .jpg, and therefore can be edited before they even enter the Photoshop environment. Different manufacturers use different file formats.	
.jpg, .jpeg	Adobe Photoshop / Adobe Illustrator, Adobe Photoshop, Adobe InDesign Developed by Joint Photographic Experts Group, hence JPEG	JPEG files have a few possible file extensions, and a wide variety of compression rates and quality settings. JPEG files are used for many applications when a small file size is required for a photographic image. JPEGs do not support any kind of transparency.	✓

CHAPTER 2: Application Basics

File Type (.extension)	Editing / Writing Program	Notes	Compressed
.gif	Adobe Photoshop / Adobe Illustrator, Adobe Photoshop Graphics Interchange Format	GIF have indexed color, and support areas of completely solid opacity or open transparency. GIFs can be made into animations, and this may be why they have held on as a format for so long (1987 to present).	✓
.png	Adobe Photoshop / Adobe Illustrator, Adobe Photoshop Portable Network Graphics	PNG was developed as a replacement for GIF. PNGs come in two varieties, PNG-8 and PNG-24. PNG-8 use indexed color, and parts of the image can be completely opaque or transparent (like GIF). PNG-24 can have levels of transparency.	✓
.tif, .tiff	Adobe Photoshop / Adobe Illustrator, Adobe Photoshop Tagged Image File Format	TIFF support layers and lossless compression. They are used in the printing industry.	✓*
.indd	Adobe InDesign	INDD file format can only be opened with Adobe InDesign, and it is very version specific. Use of .indl files can be used for older versions of InDesign.	

Introduction to Digital Media for Designers and Artists

File Type (.extension)	Editing / Writing Program	Notes	Compressed
.pdf	Adobe Photoshop, Adobe Illustrator, Adobe InDesign Portable Document Format	PDF files are designed to carry information that is platform and application independent. The reality is .pdf files can look different, and act different depending on the viewing application. However, they are still usually the best way to faithfully present a document across platforms.	✓*
.eps	Adobe Illustrator, Adobe InDesign Encapsulated PostScript	Vector object file format for faithful translation in PostScript printing.	✓*
.svg, .svgz	Adobe Photoshop, Adobe Illustrator Scalable Vector Graphics (the "z" version is compressed)	SVG files are essentially code writing an image; as such, they promise compact size, resolution independence, and text-based editing. Note: These are vector images. Photoshop will save to .svg, but it may not have all the flexibility of a .svg saved from Illustrator.	✓*

* Can also be saved without compression

Other Useful File Formats

Type	Application
.mov	QuickTime file format use for video
.mp3	Digital audio file
.mp4	Digital video file
.swf	Adobe Flash file
.fla	Editable Adobe Animate file
.html, .htm	Hypertext Markup Language; Web page file format
.css	Cascading style sheets; file for creating the look and layout of Web pages
.js	JavaScript; file for creating interactive, animated, and otherwise scripted Web pages

Quick Reference for Data Drive Formats

Format	Pros	Cons	Notes
Mac (HFS+: Hierarchical File System Plus)	Bigger than 4GB files	Windows machines cannot read it.	
Windows (NTFS: New Technology File System)	Bigger than 4GB files	Macs can usually only read it, but not write to it.	
FAT32 (32-bit File Allocation Table)	Mac OS and Windows machines can read it.	File size is limited.	
ExFAT (Extended File Allocation Table)			Designed for use on SD cards, ExFat can be read by both Macs and Windows machines. However, some other operating systems may still have issues with this format.

Introduction to Digital Media for Designers and Artists

Why Do I Need to Know This Stuff?

To be a designer or artist in the 21st century you will need to "know this stuff." Adobe software is the industry standard, and with its adoption and thorough understanding, you gain an essential foundation into all image creation software. I often say to my students, "You need to breathe Photoshop." The Adobe suite of applications will be used again and again and again. No matter which field you choose to enter, knowing the Adobe cloud of applications will be necessary; and frankly, this knowledge acquisition should be a joy. As you discover the power of these applications your ideas about what is possible in digital media and your curiosity should be peeked into all the realms of digital media, and their application to design and art.

No matter your plans as an artist or designer the Adobe Creative Cloud applications are your introduction to the essential technology you will need to know in order to navigate the field. The hypothesis of learning to use and apply the Adobe applications is foundational. This initial learning leads to necessary additional learning. This step-by-step process, I hope, leads to a wide understanding of file formats, paper sizes, screen sizes, printing processes, Web media, client relations, and the list goes on.

HOW WE USE FILES ACROSS APPLICATIONS

We have covered the two basic kinds of graphic files: vector and raster. We have talked a bit about their respective uses. Now, we will talk about the use of one kind of file in another type of application.

We begin with type—that is letters, numbers, and characters used to represent words or concepts—all dressed up (visually represented) in a font. Type is its own kind of graphic, at its most basic a vector graphic which can easily have its looks changed by changing the font in which it is typed. All of contemporary graphic design hinges on typography and the effective use of type; in fact, type—as a form of vector graphic—is in every application we are talking about. It would only follow, then, we must be able to mix and match graphic types, vector and raster, to make our design work. This is a roundabout way of thinking about vector and raster graphics, but the realization of a fluid graphic like *type* helps us understand what the programmers, engineers, and software designers had to consider when creating Adobe Photoshop, Illustrator, and InDesign. Each of these applications has its distinct niche, but (at last) they are able to handle complex integration of each other's strengths. With this said, one would never try to set a book in Photoshop, or do complex photo editing in InDesign.

© Bill Florence/Shutterstock.com

Whether we are moving a raster graphic into Illustrator or a vector graphic into Photoshop, or both into InDesign, we need to know how these applications handle the files. Can we make vector paths in Photoshop? Yes, we can. Can we use a Clipping Mask on a raster image in Illustrator? Yes, we can. Can we move either or both types of files into InDesign, and then have them create complex relationships to type? Yes, we can.

Introduction to Digital Media for Designers and Artists

The history of these applications all working together is a rocky one, but now we have a nearly seamless integration between them, as well as the other applications in the Creative Cloud.

Here I want to plant a seed in your mind. Photoshop and Illustrator can make files for use in Adobe Premiere, Adobe After Effects, Adobe Animate, Autodesk Maya, etc. Learning these foundational applications will give support to whatever ventures or direction you want to go in your work.

By now we know Adobe InDesign uses Photoshop and Illustrator files with equal ease. But, know the other applications in the Creative Cloud also use these files. Some applications, like Adobe Animate, have many ways these files can be "Imported" depending on how you want to utilize the file once you have it in the application (e.g., if you want layers to come in as layers or frames). Likewise, it can be important how you organize your file while in its native application, so Animate, After Effects, or Premiere use these files. For example, Animate looks at parsing the information in an Illustrator file in a different way dependent on layer organization. Sometimes, complexity can be an issue in this instance. I am telling you it is possible, but you will need to exercise some common sense and initiative to get the results you desire in many cases.

BASIC 3D

This is not a book about 3D applications, but I would be remiss if I did not mention the 3D abilities of Adobe Photoshop and Illustrator. With the later versions of Photoshop, the power to make computer-generated 3D objects has been greatly expanded. Photoshop allows you to extrude images and text, allowing for the creation of some pretty sophisticated objects. Likewise, Adobe Illustrator will take vector objects and extrude and bevel, revolve, and rotate, to create objects appearing 3D; however, Illustrator only has limited file output for 3D software applications. Photoshop, on the other hand, can make some pretty complex 3D scenes which have more portability to 3D applications. Ultimately, 3D applications need Adobe Photoshop and Illustrator at times to expedite some function, so if you are interested in creating 3D images, it is still vital you know Photoshop and Illustrator.

VIDEO, ANIMATION, AND EFFECTS SOFTWARE

Adobe Photoshop and Illustrator greatly add to the function of the other Adobe applications. I want to specifically address Adobe Premiere, Animate, and After Effects—video, 2D animation, and visual effects applications, respectively.

Adobe Premiere

Adobe Photoshop and Illustrator can create images for direct import into Adobe Premiere. This is very handy when one needs a still image for projects ranging from stop motion animation to logo graphics and elaborate titles. Premiere has the ability to read Photoshop layers, as a flattened image or as a variety of Premiere media arrangements, allowing the user to customize how the file is imported into Premiere for ease of use. A skilled designer or artist could create a whole motion graphics project using the tools of Photoshop then assembling and editing in Premiere.

Illustrator files can be imported into Adobe Premiere, but they come in as static images without layer options.

SEARCH TERMS

How to make video with Photoshop.

NOTE

Later versions of Adobe Photoshop have the power to create video intrinsic to the application. I do not cover this in this book, as this is intended as an introduction to Photoshop. There are many good sources for how to make video in Photoshop on the Internet. Adobe Premiere is intended to edit video, as it has only limited motion graphics capabilities. Adobe After Effects is intended to edit motion graphics and special effects, with final assembly in Adobe Premiere or Apple Final Cut Pro.

Adobe Animate

Adobe Animate was formally Flash, which is a 2D vector-based keyframe animation application. In the early days of the Internet, artists and designers yearned for a quick and easy way to create rich media interactive graphics, websites, and games for the Internet. Flash was the result. Now, Adobe Animate is still around even with the virtual collapse of Flash support for Internet devices, because there is still a need for a cool and easy application for creating fast, portable 2D animations and motion graphics across platforms. Adobe Photoshop and Illustrator both have pretty robust file support in Adobe Animate, with layers for both file systems able to be imported with a few customizations for maximum ease of use in Animate. Illustrator users please note here **layers:** Animate wants your work to be separated into layers, to have the most flexibility when imported. The use of layers in Photoshop is more likely, as it is usually necessary to get to a desired outcome.

Adobe After Effects

Of the applications I am addressing in this section, Adobe After Effects has the best cross-application support of Photoshop and Illustrator files. The nature of After Effects being a special effects and compositing tool requires it to have a lot of flexibility when it comes to importable files. When you bring Adobe Photoshop or Illustrator files into After Effects it preserves layers and allows you to bring in the files as compositions ready to go into your project.

NOTES

PART 2

Design Basics: Learning to See Again

Courtesy of The Metropolitan Museum of Art. Bequest of Marguerite H. Rohlfs, 1995.

Albert Bierstadt, *Sketch of Rocky Mountains, Canada*

Katsushika Hokusai, *Poem by Ise*

Courtesy of The Metropolitan Museum of Art. The Howard Mansfield Collection, Purchase, Rogers Fund, 1936.

Joseph Cox, Upholsterer, From LONDON, At the Sign of The Royal-Bed, In Dock-Street, near Countjies's-Market, NEW-YORK; MAKES all Sorts of Beds, both for Sea and Land; likewise, Window Curtains, Mattrasses, Easy Chairs, Sophies, French Chairs, and Chairs of all Sorts, in the newest Fashion.

Courtesy of The Metropolitan Museum of Art. Gift of Mrs. John I. Riker, 1932.

Art and Design

WHAT IS THE DIFFERENCE BETWEEN ART AND DESIGN?

John Maeda says, "Design is a solution to a problem. Art is a question to a problem." Is he right? I would, on the surface, tend to agree. But the problem of aesthetics (how things look, and their appreciation) might have a design solution, which would create a kind of recursive loop, where Maeda's art "question" is formed by the solution of an aesthetic problem. Here I am explicitly saying there is a "greater" visual design at work in art and graphic design. This is why we say, "Graphic Design" or "Industrial Design" or "Automotive Design." Design is finding a solution to a problem, *any* problem. Just to be clear, here I am going to talk about visual or graphic design, which we employ to solve visual problems and can, of course, have physical consequences (e.g., a stop sign) and a physical problem with a visual solution. Human beings are highly visual creatures. So, it should not come as a big surprise many of our design problems as a species are visual.

Graphic design takes on the visual solution for how things will look for a purpose, a cause, an objective. It is the visual tool of communication for a reason. When we look at the history of graphic design we find it is a relatively new field, essentially born in the late 19th and early 20th centuries when mass printing techniques found new precision and adaptation. Before this design renaissance the letterpress was the key tool of commerce, as gravure was expensive and slow, and lithography was still stone based. Mass advertising tended to fall to the letterpress person who did it all. With new mass media advances in printing technology and design, and layout becoming thought about with the Bauhaus in Germany and De Stijl in the Netherlands, and the need for war propaganda posters during the two World Wars, we see graphic design become a field of study, and a profession. The power of type, image, and layout were all in the hands of the graphic designer.

I think most people think of graphic designers as artists. And I do not want to dispel this notion outright. After all, we talk about "art and copy" as that moment in advertising when the artist (designer) got together with the writer to create an ad. (Please watch: *Art & Copy*, 2009 documentary film, directed by Doug Pray.) And we refer to the art director, that designer who manages and has final say over the design of the project. But, John Maeda's distillation hints to a distinct and wide gap between art and design, with both sides sometimes having a difficult time with the other. Fundamentally, I tend to make the distinction between art and design a discussion framed by utility: If something is used for a utilitarian purpose (by definition a solution to some need) then it is design; if it is used for a nonutilitarian purpose then it is art. This is not to say art is without value, as we place a lot of value in certain works of art and certain artists, but that value is determined by culture, not utility. I wish to bring these ideas up only for you to think about, and disagree with, if you have other ideas.

I have heard many designers disparage artists, and vice versa. I would point to an interrelated history and practice, and a basic foundation, which in most schools is the same. I will weigh in simply to say, "Come to all things with an open mind." And it is really important to understand the history of art and design, and realize we are on a river of continually changing tastes, which can make the future scary, the past gaudy, and yesteryear cool again. And our jobs as creative people are to think and make; and to look, make, and think again. Visual communication is capricious and prone to fits of fashion. The main thing is, we need to love to make.

SEARCH TERMS

Applied Art, Art, Arthur Danto, Design, Fine Art, Graphic Design, John Maeda, Studio Art, Visual Art

Eye charts

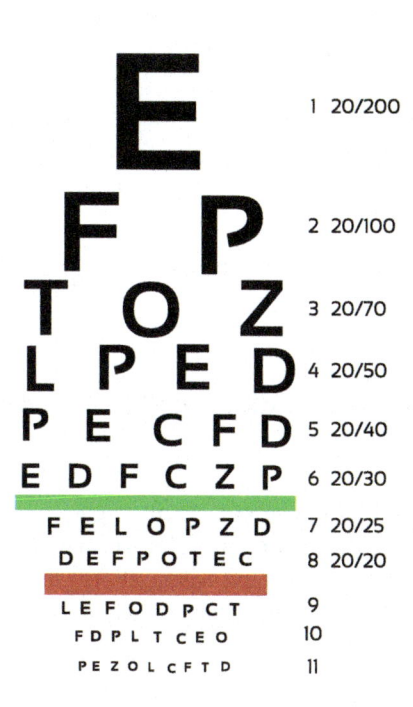

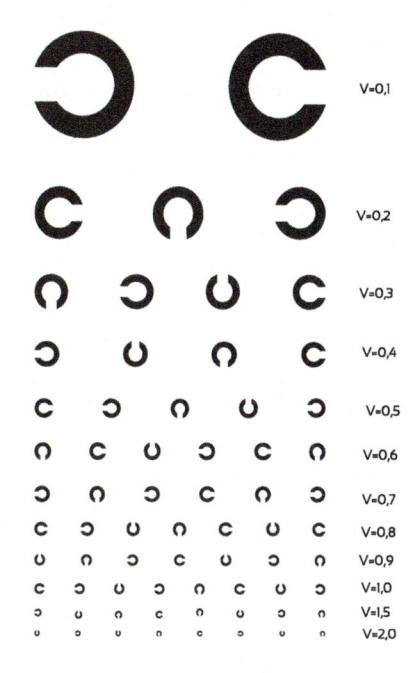

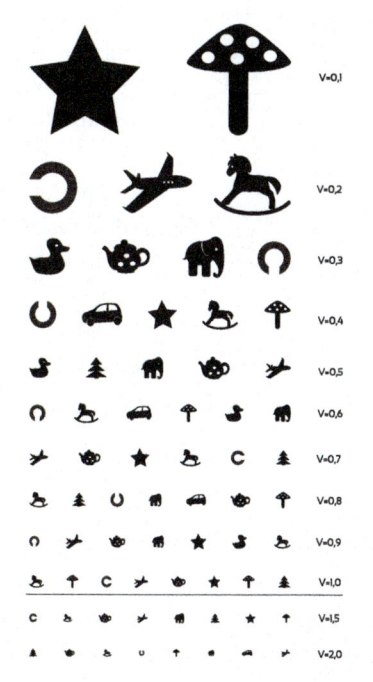

CHAPTER 4: Art and Design

49

THE GRAPHIC DESIGN PROCESS

Graphic design is visual expression employed to clearly answer a problem best answered in a visual way. Graphic design is highly creative, bringing to bear all the tools of human visuality, from image to type, in all their power.

Graphic design solves problems, and finds aesthetic solutions to practical problems. But, where do you begin?

Define the problem	Here we figure out the "what, who, where, when, and why" of our design (the "how" will come later).
Research / Resources	We gather the needed images, graphics, type, etc. We also figure out the context in which we are designing, the history, the foundational makeup, what it looks like *now*. The more we know about whatever we are designing the better solutions we will have to the problems we will encounter. Show your research.
Come up with ideas	One design is never enough, and rarely is there a number too many. Try all the ideas, even the "bad" ones. You can always edit yourself or be edited, but if we don't try all the ideas, you will not have the perspective to find the really good ones.
Refine ideas	Sometimes you will have to remove your "favorites" in pursuit of the best design for the job. Often those "discarded" designs will resurface and be used to better effect elsewhere.
Execute ideas	"Make the thing already!" Make many things—design, design, design.
Critique / Evaluate work	Open the work up to scrutiny. See how it lives in the world of other people's ideas. Note all feedback, the good and the bad. Keep your B.S. detector on "high."
Refine and fix	Take the feedback and do another pass.
Deliver / Finish	Turn in the work. On time! In the "real world" it is always better to be on time than perfect. Remember, there will almost always be changes after the work is submitted, but if you are late with the work, you WILL be fired!

Fine Art and Graphic Design

Yes, and yes! Understanding the difference will make you a better artist and/or designer. I like to think of fine art as the research group for design, like physics to engineering. Artists can take the risks, do the research, and push our level of what is "good" back and forth.

> **NOTE**
>
> Right here I want to make something very clear. Art is art as long as someone says it is. This is the beauty of art. I am not the judge of whether it is art or not art, I am only the judge of whether it is good or not. And once we get over a definition for art, we are free to enjoy liking or disliking the art in front of us.
>
> Far too often, I am told by design students that they don't like "modern" art. Horrified, I run to the computer and start unpacking the hundred or so years of modernity in all its visual output, only to find they have never really been exposed to art, "modern" or otherwise. I do my best, but I am afraid the lack of understanding is only getting more profound, so please go to a museum, see a play, travel to another country, and see the beauty of art. Please.

Entrance to the Guggenheim Museum in Bilbao, Spain.

A large installation by American sculptor Nancy Rubins. The piece, called "Pleasure Point," was displayed projecting out from the museum roof at the Museum of Contemporary Art San Diego, in La Jolla, in 2007. Photographed from the road.

Fine Art, Visual Art, Studio Art

Artist. As soon as you step into a fine art class you are an artist. I am not sure the same can be said for design. Nonetheless, what does this mean? It means humans are born with innate emotive expressive, and I would say conceptual, ability to make art. If art is asking questions, we all enter the world curious artists. This is not to say we enter as good artists, it just means *it's* there—the drive to communicate something personal. I think cultural values either cultivate and nurture these abilities or not. I am not sure we become artists, so much as we stop being artists.

Art is not easy, and creating good art is very hard. Design, at its most basic, either works or doesn't. The sign says, "stop." We stop (hopefully). What is hard in design, is what is hard in art—the aesthetics of the thing. This is why art is so important to design. It tries the "unworkable," the absurd, the "unthinkable"; it pushes culture.

Space Invader, Barcelona, Spain

How Do We Make Art?

I have talked about the design process, so what about the art process? The art process starts with asking questions. And the first question is, "How do I get my expression, thought, idea, vision into the world?" For most arts, the choice of medium answers this question. Here we find a categorification of the arts. I spent many years as a printmaker. I studied printmaking, and lived as a printmaker. At some point I found my self-categorification limiting, and with the rapid adoption of digital media, I found a new voice with the computer, manifesting itself in virtually any media from painting to sculpture, to photography to video. To back up, I studied a lot, I learned many ways of making art. I think this is why art is so hard to box up, it does not have easy solutions or necessarily right answers to the questions it asks. It requires so much searching and training to find an elegant solution, to ask hard questions, we were socialized out of being able to express in the first place.

Ultimately, the process of making art is not a formula. It does not really have right or wrong ways of being made. It does, however, like design, have aesthetic and formal concerns which are driven by cultural and social patterns of esteem and discernment—what one might call "taste" or "fashion." Art's job is to push these indices, question their efficacy, and explore new forms of conceptual and formal content. In doing this, art questions and investigates the world in which we live, and aesthetically enriches our surrounding environment.

DESIGN IN ALL THINGS

Remember this, design is in all things. We can talk about graphic design and fine art until we think we have a firm grasp on the intricacies and differences, but underpinning it all is some form of design—a design divorced from an agenda. One might be inclined to say a "natural" design. Because, as humans we have discovered [1] the Fibonacci sequence,[2] the speed of light,[3] and a few other universal contents, we have a glimpse into design in the universe. And this knowledge informs design. The golden ratio

$$\phi = (1+\sqrt{5}\,))/2 = 1.618033988749895$$

---

1. The number π is a mathematical constant, the ratio of a circle's circumference to its diameter, commonly approximated as 3.14159.
2. The Fibonacci sequence is a series of numbers where a number is discovered by adding up the two numbers before it. Starting with 0 and 1, the sequence goes 0, 1, 1, 2, 3, 5, 8, 13, 21, 34, and so forth. Written as a rule, the expression is $x_n = x_{n-1} + x_{n-2}$.
3. Approximately 3.00×10^8 m/s, approximately 186,282 mi/s in a vacuum.

54   Introduction to Digital Media for Designers and Artists

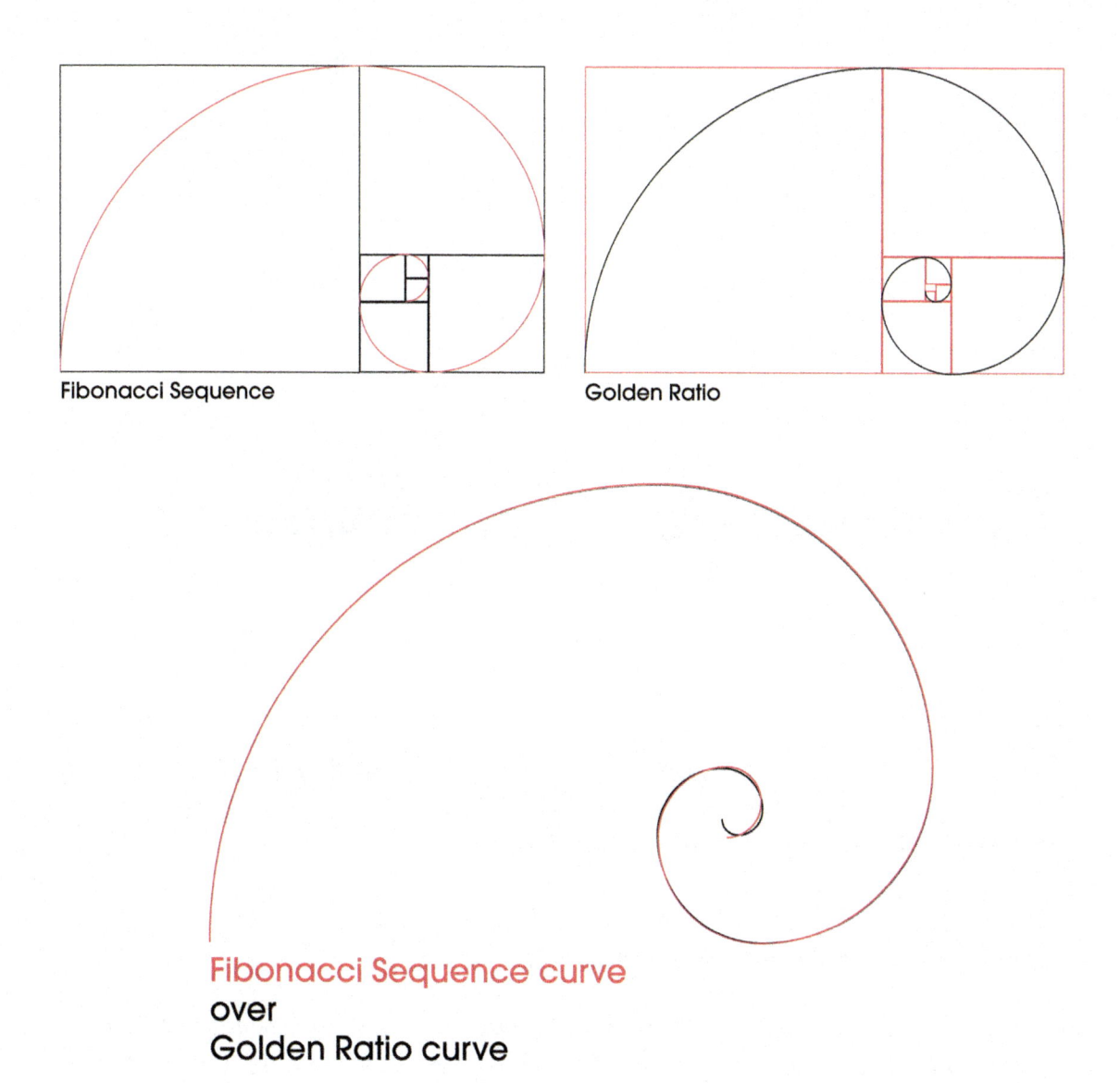

Fibonacci Sequence

Golden Ratio

Fibonacci Sequence curve
over
Golden Ratio curve

for example, is found in many natural systems, from body proportions to the inside of seashells. This basic design ratio has been used by artists, designers, and architects for millennia.

CHAPTER 4: **Art and Design**

55

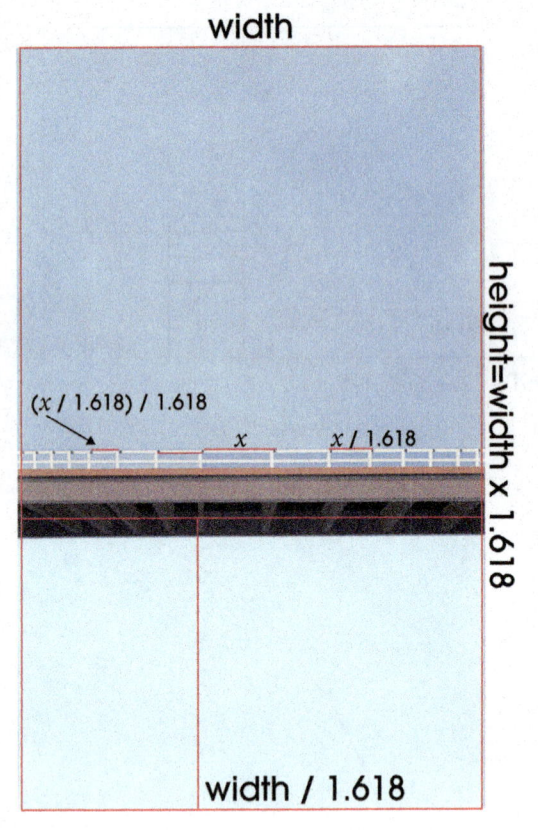

Stephen Mishol, "High" 2006, vinyl paint on paper, 22.5"x14"

We see it here in the work of artist Stephen Mishol.

This is all to say, design is bigger than a particular design field: Graphic Design, Industrial Design, Automotive Design, Architecture, Landscape Design, Product Design, Package Design, Fashion Design, Interaction Design, Urban Design, City Planning, etc. Indeed, design is also bigger than the fine arts: visual art—2D, 3D, 4D (time based); performing art—dance, theatre, film, and music; and the hybrid media, bucking classification, by the combination of media or genre. Underpinning all this output are some very concrete physical relationships, which are at use constantly, whether in practice or deliberate opposition, building up whole constituencies of philosophical endeavor, investigation, and diehard punditry. All of this, to find resonance with an artist or designer, in turn resonating with an audience to unpack and discover meaning or use.

Stamp with image by Edvard Munch

CHAPTER 4: **Art and Design**

NOTES

The Fundamental Elements

5

Having discussed art and design processes, I would be remiss in not covering the most fundamental elements of design. Here I will give you a breakdown of basic terms, most of which you will already know intuitively. Now you will have a concrete name, helping to construct a profound vocabulary of design.

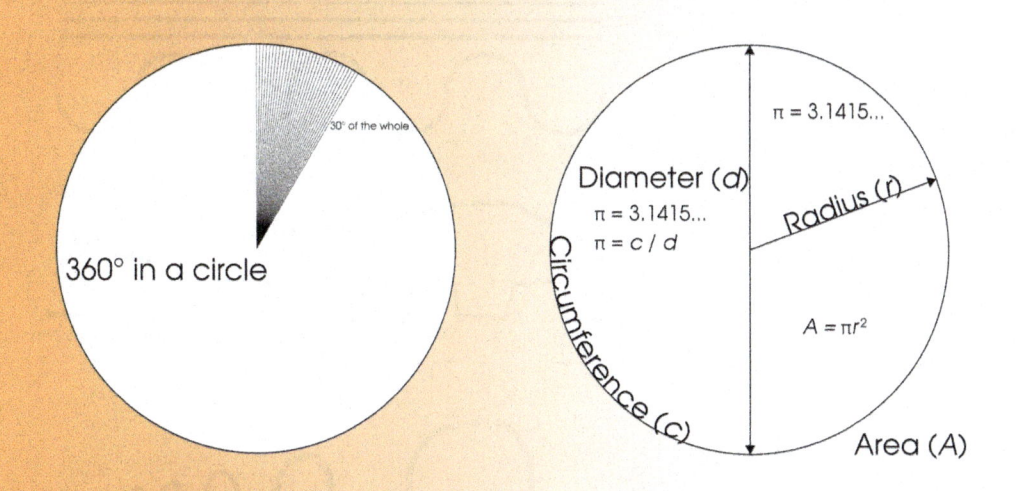

30° of the whole

360° in a circle

$\pi = 3.1415...$
Diameter (d)
$\pi = 3.1415...$
$\pi = c / d$
Circumference (c)
Radius (r)
$A = \pi r^2$
Area (A)

Degree is the measurement of an angle, so that 360 equals one full rotation. So, a circle contains 360 degrees; the sum of all the interior angles of a triangle is 180 degrees.

The circumference of a circle is the distance around the circle. The radius of a circle is the distance from the center of the circle to the edge of the circle. The diameter of a circle is the distance from one edge to another as measured through the center of the circle, or two times the distance of the radius.

Pi (Greek symbol π) is the ratio of a circle's measured circumference to its diameter and is a constant 3.1415... Therefore, one can figure the circumference of a circle by multiplying the diameter by π, or two times the radius by π.

$c = 2\pi r$ or $c = \pi d$ where c is circumference, r is radius, and d is diameter.

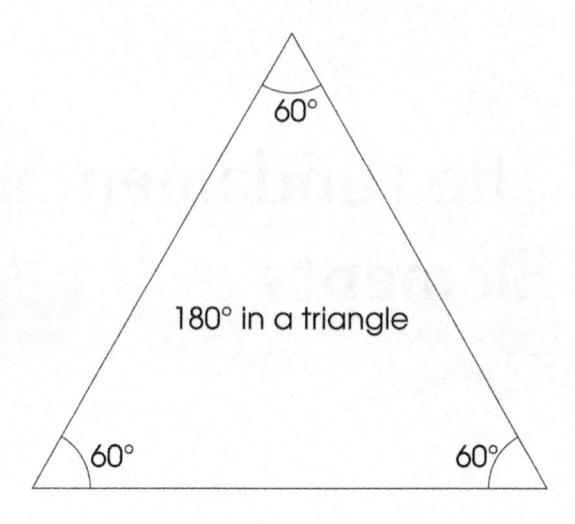

To find the area of a rectangle we multiply the height by the width. To find the area of a circle we multiply the radius by itself times π.

$$A = \pi r^2$$

LINE

The space formed between two contrasting spaces on a plane or surface, usually with some thickness and contrast distinct from either space. Line in art and design can be rectilinear or curvilinear, either straight or curved.

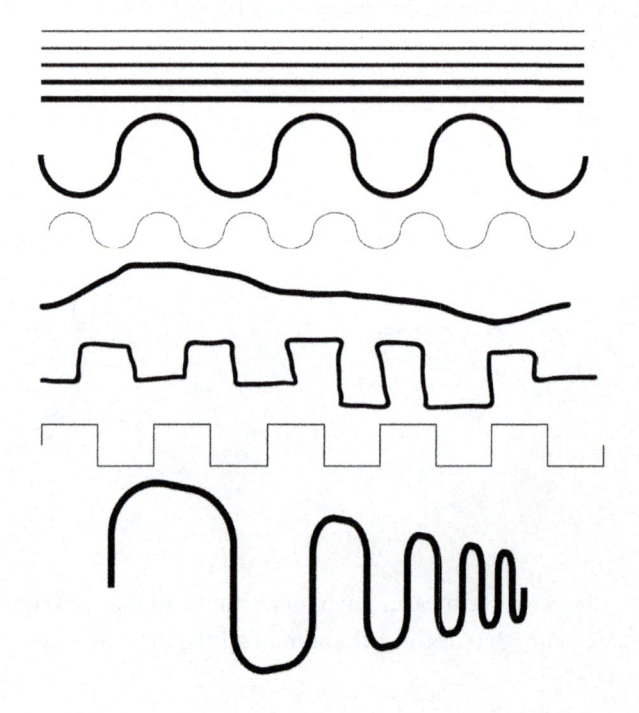

SHAPE

A shape is a two-dimensional closed geometrical figure on a plane or surface.

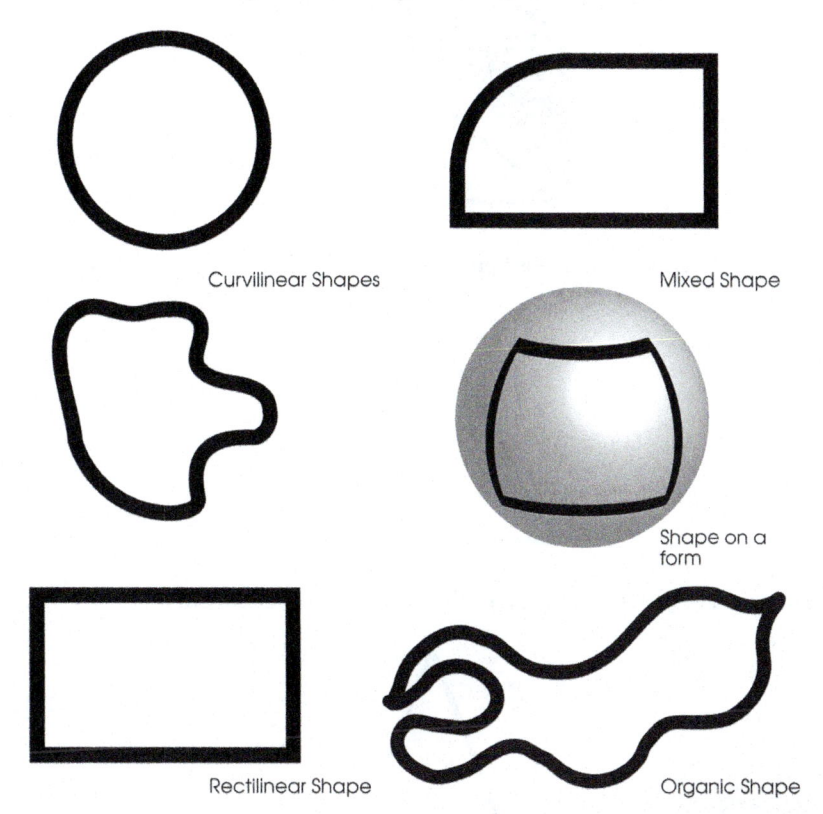

Curvilinear Shapes

Mixed Shape

Shape on a form

Rectilinear Shape

Organic Shape

Basic Shapes

Ellipse: a closed curvilinear shape, generally symmetrical in two directions.

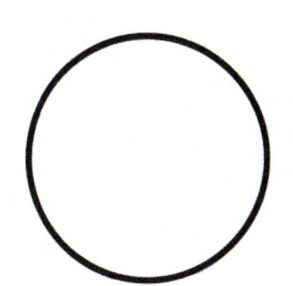

Circle: an ellipse, symmetrical in all directions.

Triangle: a three-sided rectilinear shape.

CHAPTER 5: **The Fundamental Elements**

Right Triangle: triangle with one 90-degree angle.

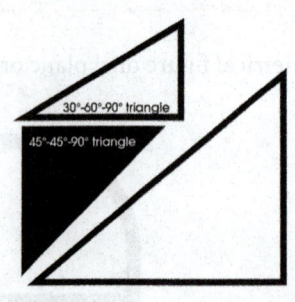

30°-60°-90° triangle

45°-45°-90° triangle

Equilateral Triangle: triangle with all sides being of equal length.

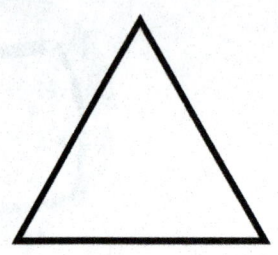

Isosceles Triangle: triangle with two equal length sides with two equal angles.

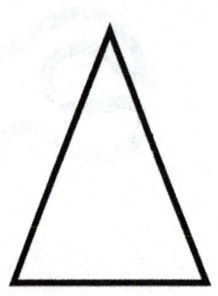

Obtuse Triangle: Triangle with one angle greater than 90 degrees.

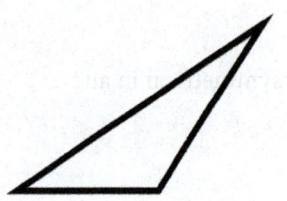

Introduction to Digital Media for Designers and Artists

Acute Triangle: triangle where all angles are less than 90 degrees.

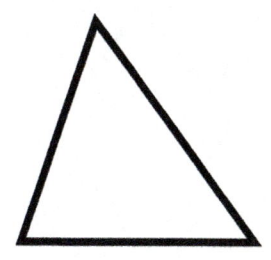

Quadrilateral: a four-sided rectilinear shape.

Rectangle: a quadrilateral with four 90-degree angles and two pairs of equal length sides.

Square: a quadrilateral with four 90-degree angles and four equal length sides.

CHAPTER 5: **The Fundamental Elements**

Rhombus: a quadrilateral with two pairs of equal inside angles and four equal length sides.

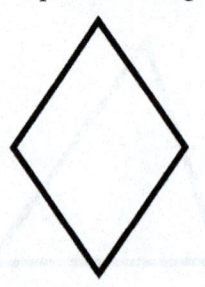

Parallelogram: a quadrilateral where opposite sides are parallel, and opposite angles are the same.

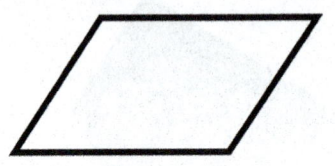

Trapezoid: a quadrilateral where two sides are parallel.

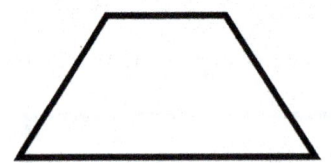

Polygons

Polygons are many-sided shapes. Here are just a few examples of polygons. Polygons can be regular convex, which is the form we are most familiar with, where all the sides are equal in length and all the corner angles are the same. But, know the term *polygon* encompasses all polygonal shapes.

Pentagon: a five-sided shape.

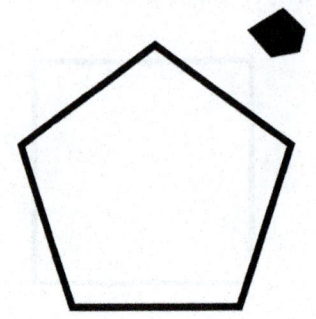

Introduction to Digital Media for Designers and Artists

Hexagon: a six-sided shape.

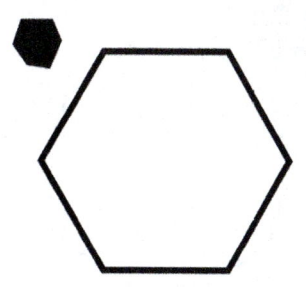

Heptagon: a seven-sided shape.

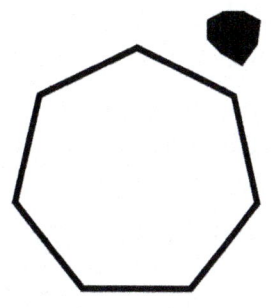

Octagon: an eight-sided shape.

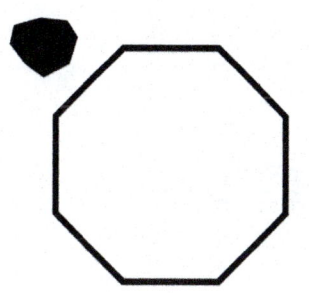

Nonagon (enneagon): a nine-sided shape.

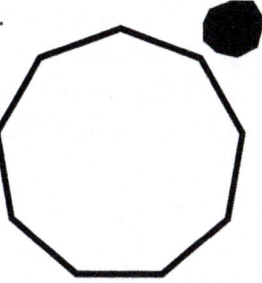

CHAPTER 5: **The Fundamental Elements**

Decagon: a ten-sided shape.

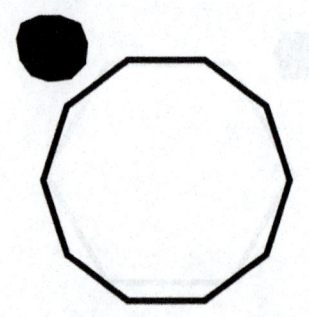

FORM

A form is a closed three-dimensional geometrical figure. For our purposes here it could either be real, like a cube of concrete sitting on the ground, or fictive, like a 3D model in a computer or a drawn representation on a 2D surface.

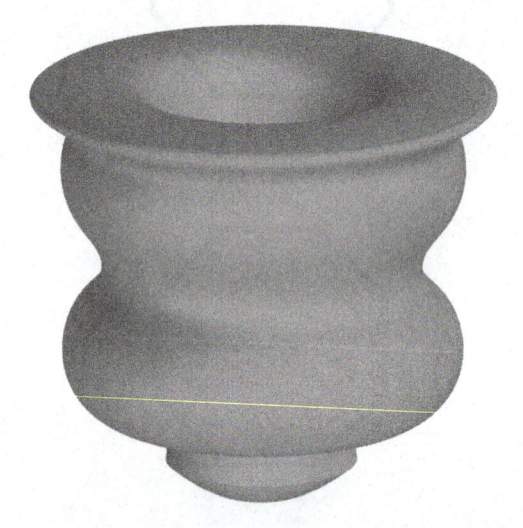

3D

When we talk about 3D forms or objects, we are speaking about an object with width, height, and depth. In the realm of fine art terms like *sculpture, installation,* or *spatial media* apply to real space. Objects or environments in this vein are experienced physically, and moved around, through, above, below, etc. These objects or environments are created to express some idea without regard to utilitarian efficacy.

Introduction to Digital Media for Designers and Artists

In the 3D design fields, like package design and industrial design, we see much the same concerns for space and human interaction with physical objects in real space. However, most of these objects are first created virtually in the computer from drawings or sketches, and then made manifest through numerous methods of output. Some examples of this are 3D printing in a plastic matrix, computer numerical control (CNC) milling device which can carve virtually any material, or other CNC devices which can form by rolling, bending, or twisting, to CNC laser and plasma cutters, which can cut nearly any shape out of nearly any material, and of course full-scale automated industrial production, just to mention a few.

© Jacomo/Shutterstock.com

© jaret kantepar/Shutterstock.com

CHAPTER 5: The Fundamental Elements

COLOR

I briefly spoke about color earlier in this book, in order for you to not be blindsided by its application in software and its fundamental use in digital media. However, there is much more to color. Its application to art and design fundamentals cannot just be distilled down to RGB versus CMYK. In art and design there is a vocabulary of color that must be understood in order to see systems of color, and communicate color intelligently to fellow designers and artists.

THE PHYSICS OF COLOR

As human beings we are only privy to about 10% of the electromagnetic radiation around us in the form of visible light and heat. This visible light manifests into perceived color in one of two ways. The first way is by reflection—light bouncing off objects, objects absorbing certain wavelengths and reflecting back others, giving the object color. This is known as subtractive color. The second way is by projection—light being emitted by an object giving the object color. This is known as additive color.

The rest of the known electromagnetic spectrum is all around us invisible to human standard vision. Examples of other wavelengths are radio waves, microwaves, and the near visible ultraviolet, and infrared. We experience the other frequencies when we cook or listen to the radio.

Additive Color

Additive color is projected color. This is not the color we learned about in grade school. The primary colors in additive color are red, green, and blue; and when all three are mixed together you get white. Additive color is the color mode of monitors, theatre lights, and the Sun. When working with media viewed on monitors or projectors, we need to be working in an RGB color space.

As you can see from the illustration, the secondary colors of additive color are a form of blue, red, and yellow. These are cyan, magenta, and yellow, which form the primary colors of subtractive color.

Subtractive Color

Subtractive color is called *subtractive* because it is the color of the material after all the other colors are absorbed, or subtracted, from the light reflected. I like to think about it as reflected color, as this makes a nice symmetry with "projected" color (additive color). At its heart, subtractive color is the color of pigments, dyes, and inks. It is the color we learn as children, with the primary colors red, yellow, blue, and the secondary colors—the colors, when two primary colors are mixed—orange, green, purple (or violet).

CHAPTER 5: **The Fundamental Elements**

This is the color wheel we learn as children. As the science of color progressed the printing industry figured out process color, with the primary colors being cyan, magenta, and yellow. With these three colors, various mixing processes would provide an approximation of most fully saturated colors, as well as most tints, by using the white of the paper. But, something was missing. If you mixed full cyan with full magenta, with full yellow, the best you would get is a dark brown. Yes, you guessed it, black. With the addition of black to the printing process, a full range of greys allowed for tints, tones, and shades of color, as well as black and rich black (the mix of 100% CMYK).

CMYK is the color space of printing and pigment mixing.

PRINTING AND COLOR CREATION

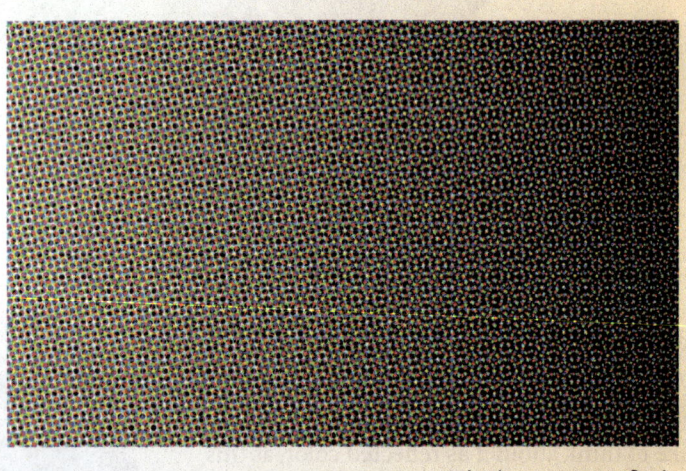

Color in printing can come about in a few forms. Continuous tone involves printing with a mixed color, displaying the color you get. In continuous tone printing you might have a specified color from a system such as Pantone. Halftone printing uses a dot screen, printing a process color next to another dot screen printing another process color. In this way, the colors are mixed in close proximity by our eyes. With electrostatic and inkjet printing we still have dots but the screens are replaced by algorithms, which closer approximate the continuous tones of digital photography (more on printing later in the book).

Introduction to Digital Media for Designers and Artists

Primary Colors	Color Space Abbreviation	Type of Color
Red, Yellow, Blue	RYB	Subtractive
Cyan, Magenta, Yellow, Black	CMYK	Subtractive
Red, Green, Blue	RGB	Additive

Hue

Hue is the perceived color of the visible spectrum (e.g., red, blue, green).

Embodied in hue is the temperature of color: warm to cool, from red to blue. This has physical as well as psychological implications. Warm colors are literally "warmer" as they reflect more of the heat-producing electromagnetic spectrum than the cooler colors. We also tend to think about reds as being passionate, fiery, hot-headed, while as we move toward the blue, we calm down; we think of blue sky and oceans.

Yellow tends to play the spoiler in this interplay of color, but even yellows are warmer or cooler depending on how much red or blue is involved as it moves toward orange or green.

Value

The value of a color is the lightness or darkness of the color. In pigment color (subtractive color) this translates to the amount of white, black, or grey a color has in it. These are broken down as follows:

Tint
A tint is made by adding white to a hue.

CHAPTER 5: **The Fundamental Elements**

Tone
A tone is made by adding black to a hue.

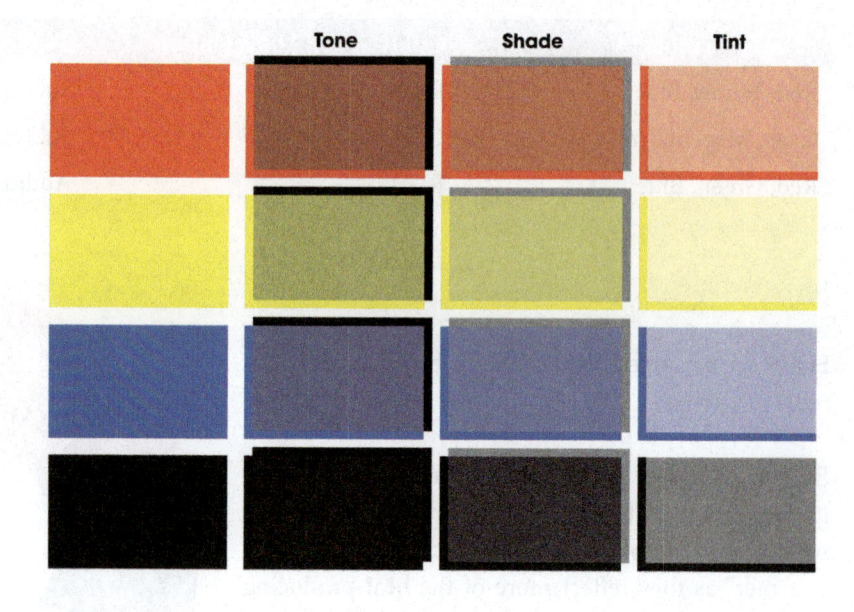

Shade
A shade is made by adding grey to a hue.

Introduction to Digital Media for Designers and Artists

Saturation

Saturation is how bright or intense a color is perceived relative to other colors. In physical terms, the saturation of a color is determined by its closeness to one wavelength of light. In design and fine arts terms words like *clean, bright, intense* are used, as opposed to *dull, muddy, dark,* etc. A saturated color is bright and intense (really, you will know it when you see it, hopefully).

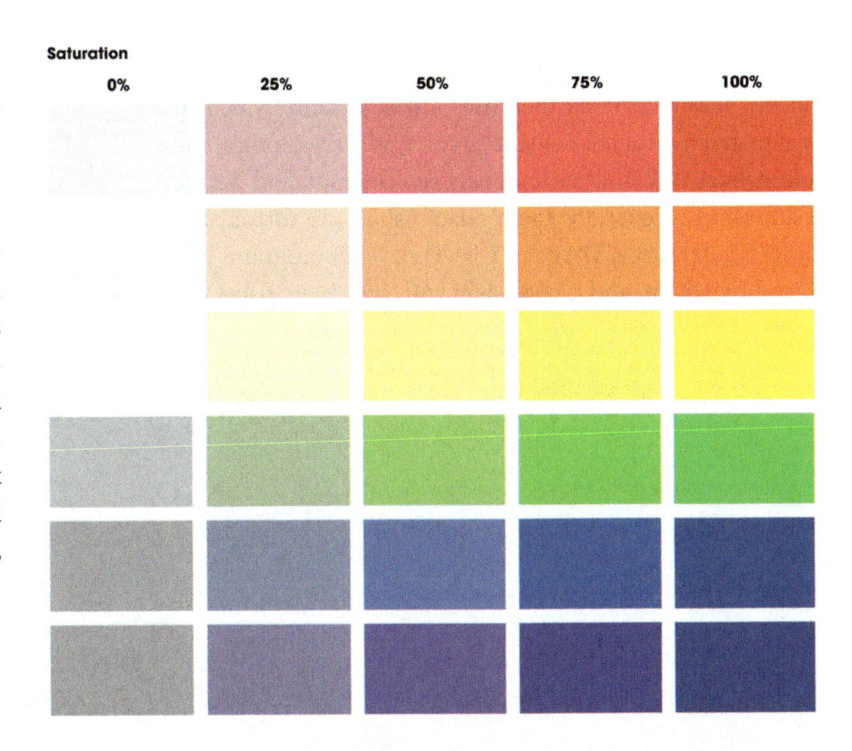

Saturation
0% 25% 50% 75% 100%

In applications you will often be looking at HSB (hue, saturation, brightness) color, with hue being the color (red, blue, green, yellow, orange, etc.), saturation being the purity of the hue, and brightness being the darkness or lightness of the hue. This is the default color space of Adobe Photoshop in the color picker.

CHAPTER 5: **The Fundamental Elements**

COLOR SCHEMES

As humans endeavored to put colors next to each other, it quickly became evident there was a design sense which in turn had a physical relationship to color. When we look at the color wheel, we can draw lines between colors to find design relationships. Generally, these relationships are formulated for RYB color space. The color wheel is used in programs like Adobe Illustrator, and is consistent with any color spaces.

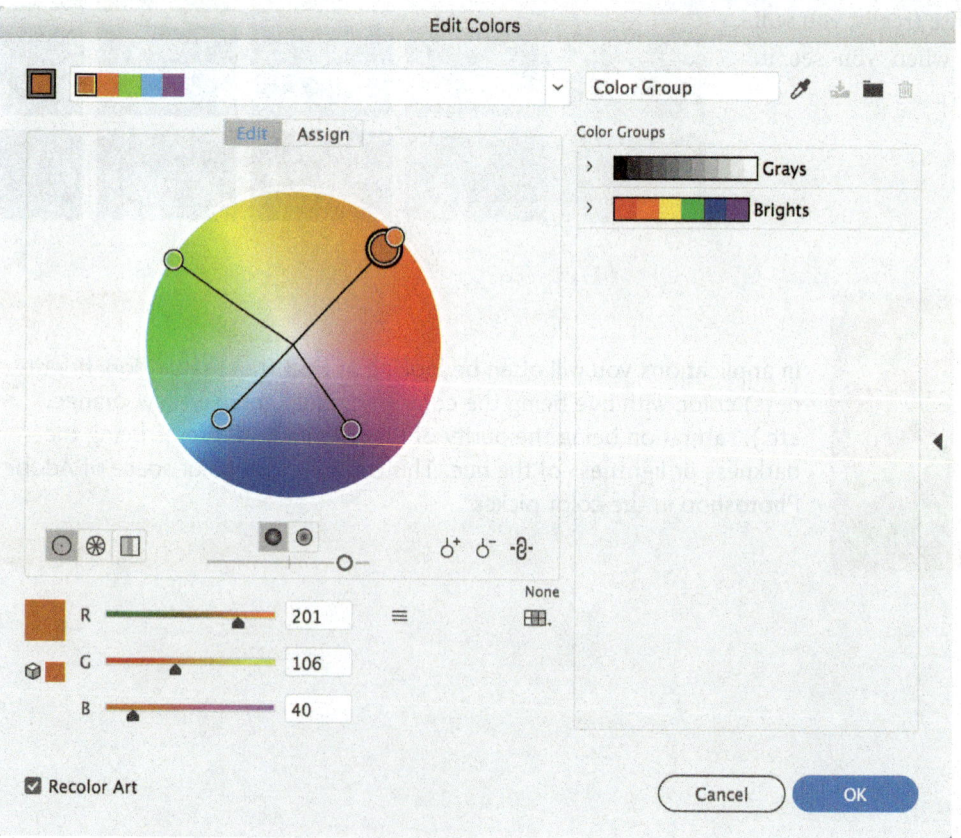

Here are a few of these codified relationships.

Introduction to Digital Media for Designers and Artists

Complementary

Complementary, or complementary opposite, colors are basically the colors directly opposite the other on the color wheel.

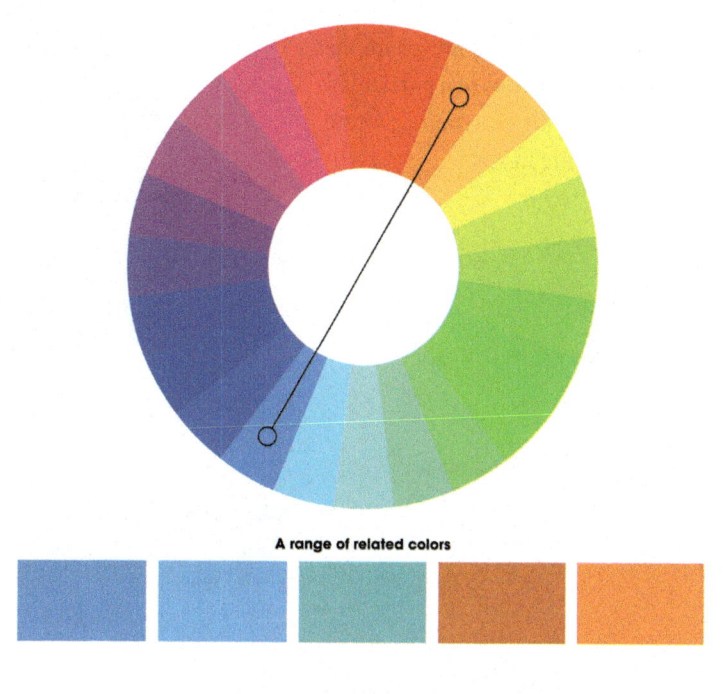

A range of related colors

Analogous

Analogous colors are next to each other on the color wheel.

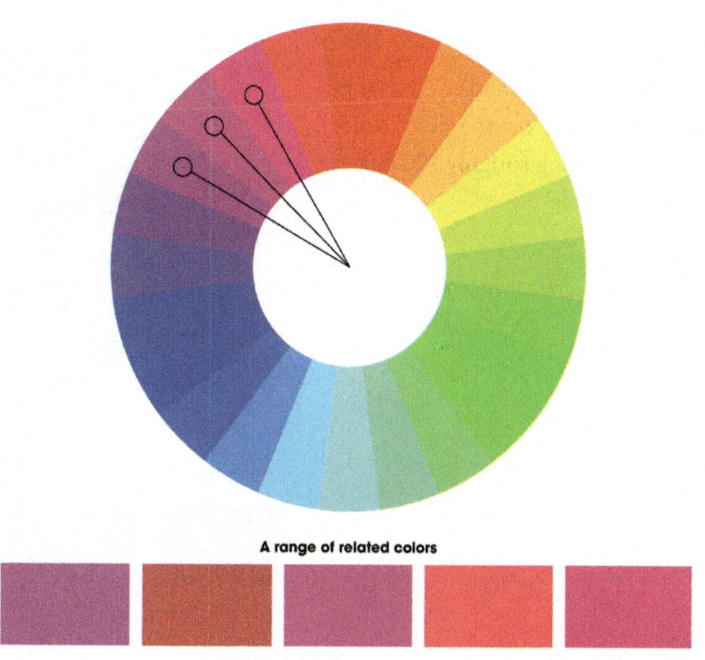

A range of related colors

CHAPTER 5: **The Fundamental Elements**

Monochromatic

Monochromatic colors are made up of the tints and shades of a particular hue—a color with a certain amount of black or white in it.

A range of related colors

Triadic

Triadic colors are made by a triangular relationship on the color wheel; each color being roughly 120 degrees from the other.

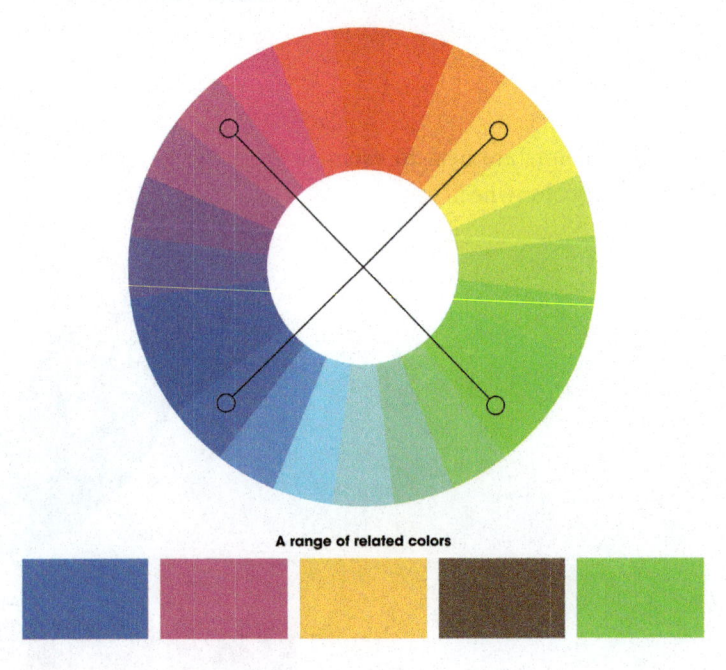

A range of related colors

Tetradic

Tetradic, like triadic, color is a simple geometric form relationship, this time a square; each color being 90 degrees from the other. This relationship could also be a rectangle, as a variation.

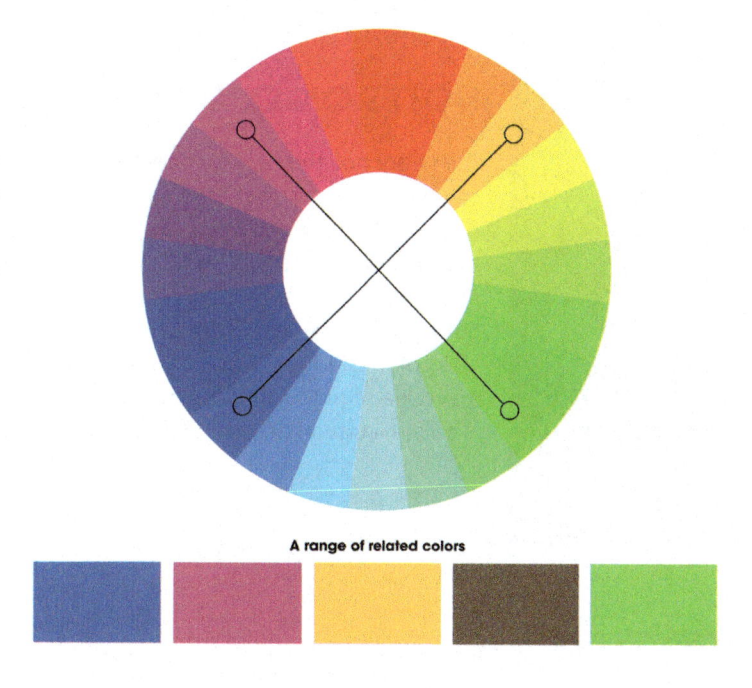

A range of related colors

Pentagram

Pentagram color also exploits a geometric relationship, with each color being 72 degrees from the last, totaling five colors in a pentagonal relationship.

A range of related colors

CHAPTER 5: **The Fundamental Elements**

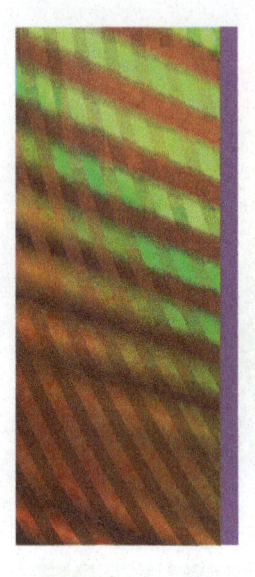

NOTES ON COLOR SCHEMES

These are not the only color schemes in the world. These relationships can be modified and shifted to serve a need or a direct purpose. I would be loath to think one might be limited by this information. Color is as plastic as any other art and design tool. I can imagine the wall-to-wall green, red, and brown shag carpeting of my childhood home in the 1970s, but I would have a hard time buying it in the 21st century…for now.
Use color as a tool to solve your problem or express your thought, not as a shackle of physical relationships or even "good taste." Color and its use is a fluid, cultural practice. Please remember this.

TEXTURE

Texture is the irregularities of a surface giving the perception of different materials, or at the most basic level: smooth to rough, matte to glossy, and so forth.

I have a painter friend who would be upset I included texture in the lexicon of basic design terms, as "texture" is created by all the other terms, as he sees it; it is not an element unto itself. However, when we get into the simulation of reality, as with 3D modeling, we cannot help but speak about and include texture. As well, a sculptor deals with texture as it pertains to real materials (wood, metal, stone, etc.). The idea of texture is built up from the modulation of line, shape, form, and color; this is an interesting idea, especially for a 3D modeler

© Rodin Anton/Shutterstock.com

Introduction to Digital Media for Designers and Artists

who is not dealing with real materials but only the perception associated with those materials, as simulated by the computer. So much of our perception of things is associated with the texture of the world, but remember this visually is just modulation of the basics of form; we do not experience texture with vision, but with touch.

SPACE

We don't make art and design in a vacuum. We need to talk about space. Space in art and design can be real or fictive, it can be 2D, 3D, or even 4D when we are talking about time-based media. I want to distill space down to the terms artists and designers have been working with and against for…well, since humans were working on cave walls.

Designers and artists throw around the word *space* with a casual freedom, which belies its quintessential importance to making anything, and especially making something good or at least interesting.

In this section I give you ideas of space intended for an essentially 2D medium, as this book is intended mainly for art and design students working in flat media. This is not to say these are not of importance to the 3D art and design disciplines, just that my examples will be geared toward 2D space.

Composition

Basically, the composition is the arrangement of elements on the constraining matrix. This matrix could be a piece of paper, or a field of grass in three dimensions. A cinematographer deals with the composition in the field of vision of the camera. A painter deals with the composition on a canvas. We, as artists and designers, strive to create compositions of interest and intent. We don't (usually) strive for imbalance, disharmony, or disjointedness—unless perhaps for a conceptual reason.

Dave Hickey in his book, *The Invisible Dragon* (Art Issues Press, 1993), makes a compelling argument for "beauty," which he argues is found in the form and finish of a work of art, perhaps disassociated from its underlying meaning, but still part-and-parcel attached; creating work which may have meaning disagreeable to a type of viewer, but in a form which checks all the boxes of what that viewer has normally associated with the beautiful, the well composed, and generally has the clothes of elegance. Hickey's argument is, that work is powerful (if, possibly controversial). In the decades since Hickey's masterful thesis, we have found this playing out in art and design time again, sometimes to challenge us as viewers and our preconceptions, other times to sell an idea, perhaps abhorrent, in the clothes of beautiful design.

Composition, and the elements of art and design, are the "invisible dragon," creating the visually compelling images, asking the important questions, and solving the important visual problems, to make ideas look great; sometimes selling us a vision we might otherwise reject. I cannot emphasize enough the power of design, to change the world; I will optimistically look for the better.

Composition has some classical forms, based on a structure of balance and unity, and leading the viewer's eye through the work.

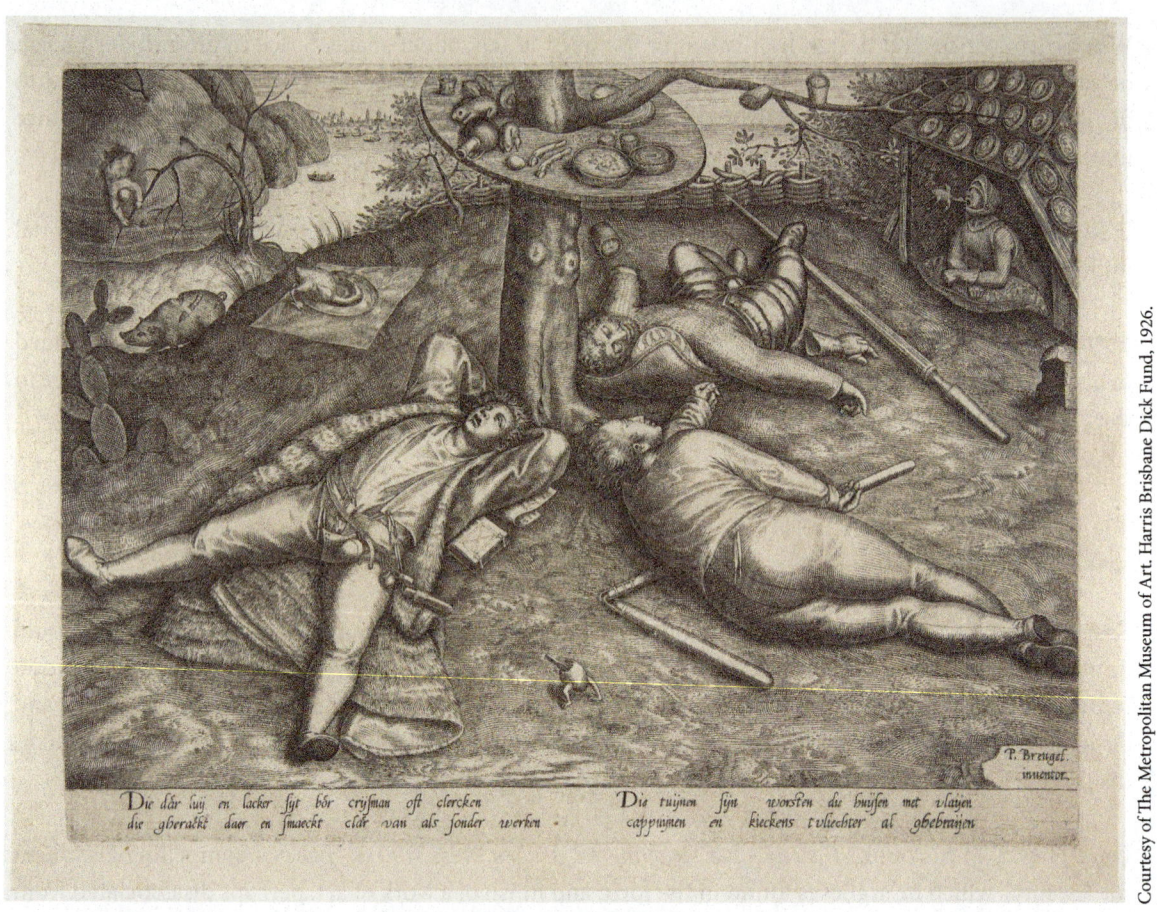

Attributed to Pieter van der Heyden, *The Land of Cockaigne*

Courtesy of The Metropolitan Museum of Art. Harris Brisbane Dick Fund, 1926.

Introduction to Digital Media for Designers and Artists

Figure–Ground Relationship

The figure–ground relationship at its most basic is a way to emphasize the position of an element or elements in a space either real or fictive, bound by a matrix of a given medium. This relationship builds by a perception of the object, and the surrounding space and the interplay between them. From this relationship we discover the other compositional relationships.

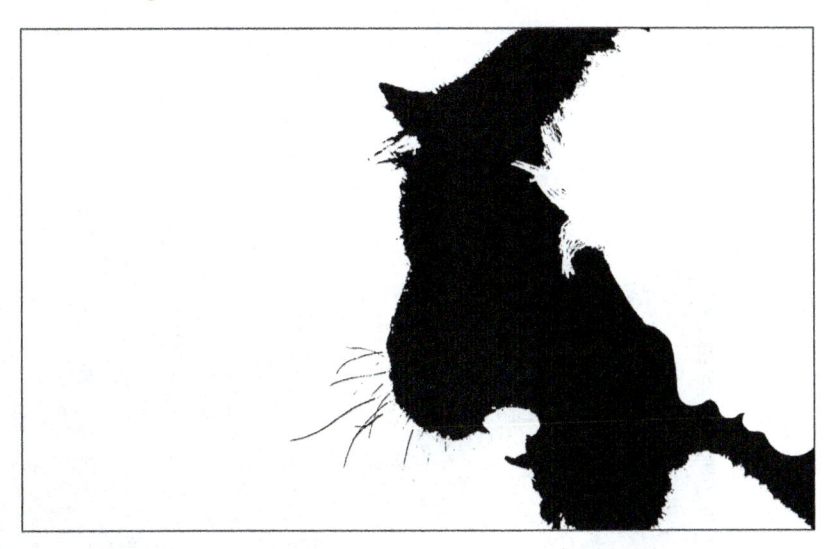

Negative Space, Positive Space

Negative space is the space around an object. In design the negative space can build meaning, hold content, and construct another way of seeing. This is important for visual literacy, and the understanding of a figure on a ground, which is a basis of building fictive depth in a 2D medium.

CHAPTER 5: **The Fundamental Elements**

Foreground, Middleground, Background

The relationship of multiple objects at multiple distances to the image plane, one "in front" of the other is the basis for the foreground, middleground, background relationship. This idea in a medium like photography seems self-explanatory, but in practice we find the idea much more complex, especially across media. But, sum it up to say, one thing is in front of another, which is in front of the "background." In design, as well as in applications, we call these layers information along the *z* axis (in an *x, y, z* coordinate system).

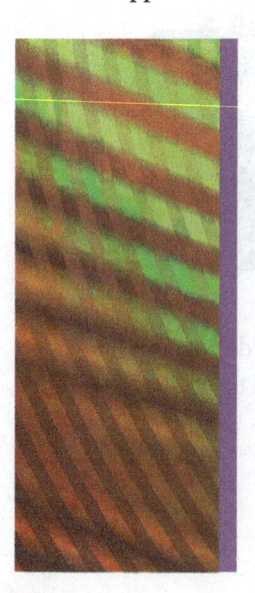

x, y, z coordinate system as used in Web and graphic design, where *x* is the horizontal axis, *y* is the vertical axis, and *z* is the depth axis. The start of zero varies from application to application. For example, in designing for the Internet, zero in the x and y starts in the upper left corner and increases both down and left, and terms like *z-index* are used to set depth. This is different from a traditional Cartesian coordinate system.

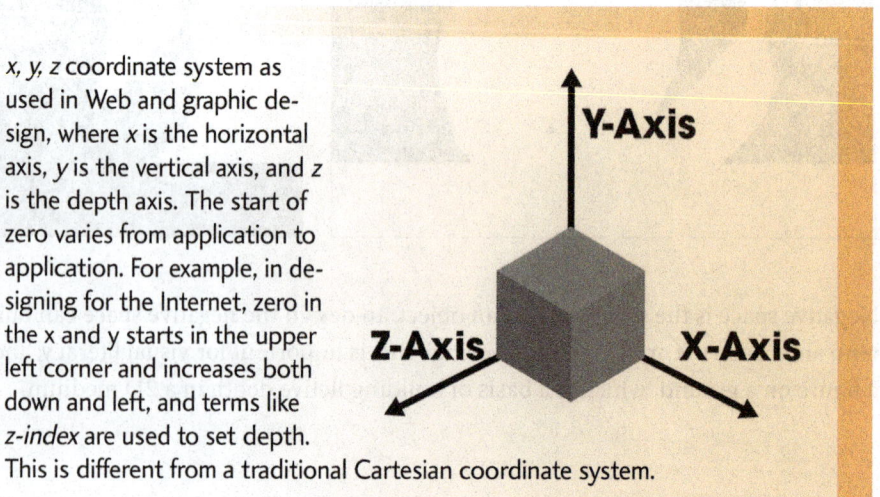

Introduction to Digital Media for Designers and Artists

SEARCH TERMS

Cartesian coordinate system

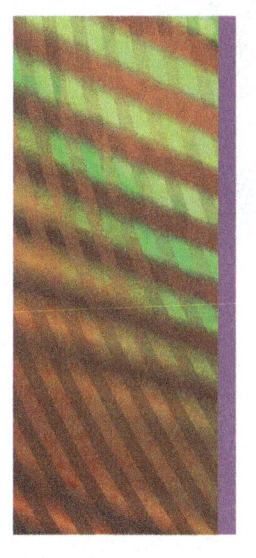

PICTURE PLANE

The imaginary plane located between the viewer and the object (subject) being viewed; it is generally coexistent with the surface of the 2D medium being used, paper, canvas, monitor, etc.

Perspective

When we begin a discussion on perspective, we must realize all the word implies. We are talking about a point of view, a position of the viewer (either real or fictive) to a scene or object. Perspective in art and design is generally concerned with the representation of a 3D space on a 2D surface. We, as human beings (generally), see in a near 180-degree arc, stereoscopically—able to see depth and solidness. To represent this experience on a 2D surface is at best an approximation, a mathematical abstraction. As with other mathematical endeavors there are some basic rules to these creations.

Fra Angelico, *The Crucifixion*

Courtesy of The Metropolitan Museum of Art. Maitland F. Griffis Collection, Bequest of Maitland F. Griggs, 1943.

CHAPTER 5: The Fundamental Elements

One-Point Perspective

One-point perspective occurs when the objects being represented are at right angles to the picture plane and each other, and the viewpoint is such that all the horizontal lines converge in a single vanishing point. In the case of one-point perspective the vertical lines are **always** vertical, this is to say straight up and down.

Two-Point Perspective

Two-point perspective occurs when the objects being represented are being viewed from a position in which only the vertical lines are parallel to the picture plane, allowing the horizontal lines to vanish in two directions, at two distinct points. In this perspective the viewer can **only** observe objects positioned between the two points—trying to draw or create objects outside of the two points will result in a breakdown of the system. In two-point perspective vertical lines are still **always** vertical, straight up and down.

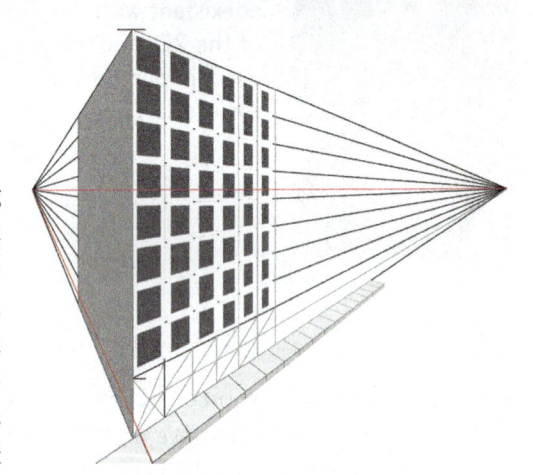

Three-Point Perspective

Three-point perspective occurs when neither the vertical lines nor horizontal lines of an object are parallel to the picture plane. This view assumes a position either slightly above or below the object, which allows the viewer to see the object receding into space in three dimensions. In the case of three-point perspective the only true vertical line would be positioned in the exact middle of the system,

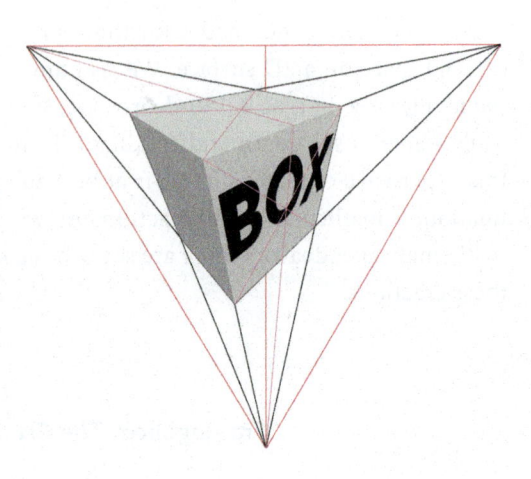

Introduction to Digital Media for Designers and Artists

otherwise all vertical lines will vanish into the third point. There are rules about the relationship of the three points to each other, as the angle formed will determine the amount of foreshortening; this angle cannot be greater than 90 degrees and still represent a realistic perspective. Additionally, like two-point perspective, every object in your scene must be contained within the triangle formed by the vanishing points.

Foreshortening

Foreshortening is the perception of objects becoming shorter as they approach perpendicular to the picture plane.

Battista Franco, *Lamentation of the Virgin*

Courtesy of The Metropolitan Museum of Art. The Elisha Whittelsey Collection, The Elisha Whittelsey Fund, 1954.

SEARCH TERMS

Four-Point Perspective, Zero-Point Perspective

Trompe l'oeil

Trompe l'oeil is a French term meaning "deceive the eye." This term was originally used to describe a form of painting, so naturalistic, as to fool the viewer into "believing" the scene to be real. With the advent of photography, this term has been expanded to include optical illusions of all sorts.

Gerrit van Honthorst, *Musical Group on a Balcony*

© Everett - Art/Shutterstock.com

CHAPTER 5: **The Fundamental Elements**　　85

Painted building facade in Madrid, Spain

Compositional Ideas and Design Principles 6

I have talked about the fundamental building blocks of images and objects in visual art and design. Now we will talk about putting them to work. The aesthetics of art and design are in constant cultural flux. As we go through time, the way we think about the world of visual culture changes as culture itself changes. Why would we expect anything else? I have talked about the basic material of visual images. A pentagon is always a pentagon, blue is always blue. Now, we will embark on a journey to figure out how we use a pentagon, and the color blue; and remembering always, these are culturally pinned.

For over 40,000 years humans have been creating images. In this time we have constructed myths, legends, visual patterns, mathematically important numbers, natural observations, stellar patterns, lunar motions, and general cultural fashions. Your job as an artist or designer is to decode and encode all this history of human visual output into something resonating in your time and place in culture—presumably *your* culture, but maybe even another; this is difficult. What follows here is a few of the guides and strategies others have used in forging paths through and to visual communication. Remember, these are only ideas of how to do something, ultimately you will have to find your own way to make, and in this making you will find other modes, or even make new ones. The main thing is to be fearless and experimental in your quest for mastery.

COMPOSITIONAL IDEAS

Artists and designers have been looking at the way we see, understand, and relate to visual communication for the last 40,000-plus years. These are just a few of the more talked about compositional ideas in the field. Again, I give examples here so you are familiar with common ideas in the field, not so you are trapped by history into any concrete working model; your model should be *yours*.

Rule of Thirds

The "Rule of Thirds" builds images with a more dynamic composition based on visual asymmetry along lines dividing the image into nine equal parts, a 3 x 3 grid. This idea is prevalent in photography and filmmaking (cinematography). Proponents of this idea look to it to produce more dynamic and visually engaging images, over a purely center-focused composition.

Rule of Space (Nose Room)

The "Rule of Space" is sometimes referred to as "nose room." It is a compositional idea which leaves room in front of the subject. The idea is one of "comfortable" space. If the subject has the edge of the image close to the front of the subject, proponents of this idea site the

Introduction to Digital Media for Designers and Artists

"discomfort" of the subject empathically affecting the viewer. This also follows with moving subjects, where, without space in front, the subject would seem to exit the compositions "too fast." This is also referred to as "lead room."

Rule of Odds

The idea of the "Rule of Odds" contends, humans are more comfortable looking at an odd number of subjects. The idea comes from a desire to be more naturalistic in composing images; where even numbers tend to fall into symmetrical relationships, which tends to occur less in nature. This idea may seem a stretch, and can be highly subjective, but many successful images utilize this idea.

Rhythm

Rhythm, unlike the "rules," consists in every image to some degree. The idea of subjects dispersed in relation to one another, forming a rhythm, is used to create visual interest and give relational meaning.

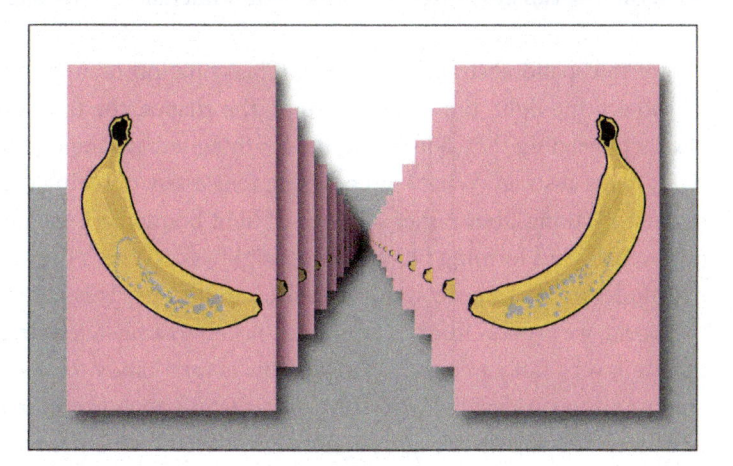

CHAPTER 6: Compositional Ideas and Design Principles

Leading the Viewer

"Leading the viewer" is simply placing geometrical compositional elements in the image in order to direct the viewer's attention to a particular element in the work. Often time in sophisticated old master paintings we will see a triangular leading of the viewer, so a cycle is formed, engaging the viewer in a looping composition—many times the viewer seems to be "included" in this compositional process; it is not unlike cinematography from a first-person point of view. In time-based media, we see this often. Its application to static art and design is more difficult, but can be very compelling when accomplished well.

ABSTRACTION

Abstraction is the elephant in the room. Abstraction as most people use the term, just means nonrepresentational or not naturalistic. But, abstraction in fine art of the mid-20th century was about taking from the naturalistic, certain elements, pairing down the image, finding "new" forms, but still rooted essentially in that form; the term was more like, to be abstracted from something. We now causally use the term to mean anything which does not immediately look like something.

I want to expand abstract here to the representation of anything. When you look closely at an object or subject, the light, the color, the lines, the shapes, the forms of the object or subject are essentially abstract; meaning they don't look like anything, except the light bouncing off the subject, which recursively looks abstract. What I am pointing to is a way of seeing the world, not as a series of symbols with distinct meanings, but rather a bunch of light bouncing here and there, reflecting, hitting the backs of our eyeballs and forming pictures. You might ask, "What's the difference?" The difference is in the symbol model we assume we *know* the world around us. This is really good for survival. In shorthanding the world, we process information much faster, so a tiger, a bear, a large mountain cat, gets processed in the brain very fast and signals *danger*. This is very handy for a slow bipedal terrestrial dwelling primate who wants to survive; likewise, for a driver who knows the shorthand of a red octagon sign, and comes to a stop. We, as artists and designers don't need to see the world this quickly. We can take our time and look at things as they are, not as we *think* they are; and in this way really *see*, not just assume. And abstraction is at the heart of seeing, even—and especially—seeing and making the representational. Of course, once we understand the representational, we can then abstract from it to myriad images, styles, fashions, movements, times, and desires; unlocking your creative and persuasive best; encoding symbols with profound meaning. Basically, in order to really see something you must reduce it down to just the light being reflected off of it, disregarding what you *think* it is. This is abstract, the image you see when you do this is just a bunch of light, maybe in a pattern, maybe not, but once you assemble this light into an image—now of your creation—you can step back and see the subject, now moved to representation.

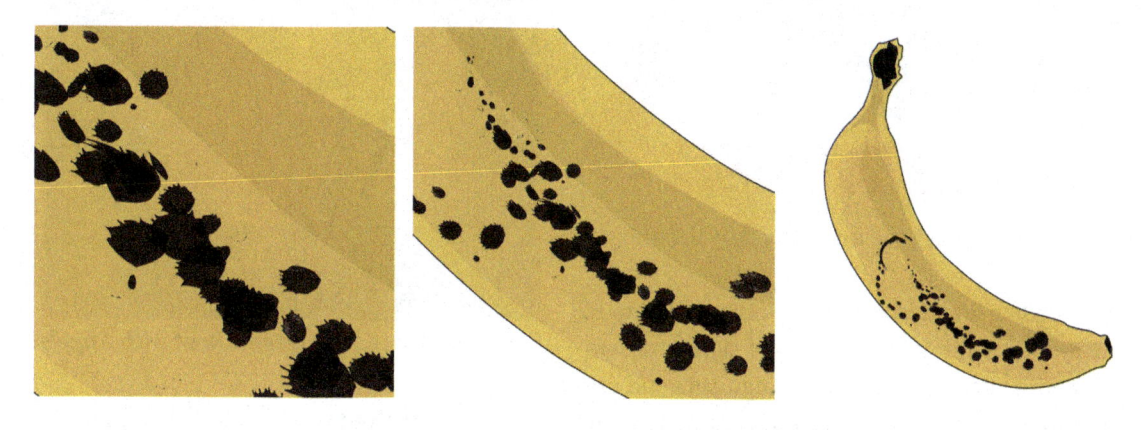

THE SYMBOL

After talking about looking at the world as essentially abstract light (see earlier discussion on abstraction), we need to add balance to one visual system, which is very good at encoding information through a human into compelling images. But, "compelling" images without meaning within context are not truly compelling in the whole. We might be awed by the virtuosity of reproduction, but we will eventually contextualize even this into systems of meaning: symbols. Artists and designers are constantly using symbols to build and control meaning, so a firm cultural understanding of their use is essential. A symbol—for our purposes—is an image, sign, or graphic which has a generally agreed upon cultural meaning, which can be decoded. Some symbols have near universal meaning, like a red octagon, while others strive to be understood by reducing fundamental imagery into pictographic situations.

CHAPTER 6: **Compositional Ideas and Design Principles**

Others are only meant to be understood by the initiated.

When encoding and decoding symbols, we tend to fall on the tools of semiotics, the study of signs and symbols. Semiotics deploys the tools of linguistics and psychology, in order to study the meaning, as well as how this meaning evolved.

Édouard Manet, *The Dead Christ with Angels*

DESIGN PRINCIPLES

At the root of visual communication is a basic ordered design. For myself, I find design more complicated, transcendent, and culturally biased than can really be boiled down into a set of discretely defined terms. However, what we gain from talking about these ideas is valuable; and designers, very rightly, should value constraints.

The following principles are to give us a starting point, a reference, and a common language to help explain our visual ideas in words.

Unity and Harmony

When we talk about unity and harmony we are seeing the elements of the image in a place of visual comfort. We might say something like, "all those belong together." There are tools or strategies within this principle for creating or finding unity and harmony.

Tool/Strategy	Definition	Image
Rhythm (consistent)	Rhythm, at the service of unity and harmony, is achieved when visual repetition is interrupted at a consistent interval.	
Proximity	Proximity is the grouping together of objects to create a sense of belonging together.	

CHAPTER 6: **Compositional Ideas and Design Principles**

Continuation	Continuation is the creation of a visual element in the composition across distinct areas of the image.	
Repetition	Repetition is created by repeating visual elements in the composition.	
Similarity	Similarity is like repetition, while only taking some of the visual references from object to object, enough so we would find them similar.	

Introduction to Digital Media for Designers and Artists

Balance

We understand balance when it comes to a teeter-totter on the playground or a scale at the doctor's office. For visual communication, it is pretty much the same—one side of the image equals the other side of the image. We can understand balance in certain ways.

Tool/Strategy	Definition	Image
Symmetry	Having an equal amount of elements of the same type on each side of the image	
Asymmetry	Having an amount of elements of various shapes and sizes which equate to a net equilibrium	

CHAPTER 6: **Compositional Ideas and Design Principles**

Radial Symmetry	Having a circular spread of elements with net equilibrium	
Crystallographic Symmetry	Having an all-over distribution of elements with a net equilibrium	

Hierarchy

Hierarchy in design guides the viewer to the most important or general information to the more specific. If we consider a movie poster as an example of hierarchy, generally the image is the largest image, then the title, then the starring actors, and then finally the director, producers, supporting actors, movie studio, etc. This is a hierarchy of *weight*. Here is list of types.

Introduction to Digital Media for Designers and Artists

Tool/Strategy	Definition	Image
Weight	The size of the object peaks the viewer's attention first, cluing to object importance.	**IMPORTANT** **LESS IMPORTANT** **Even less important, but the actual content.** **Even less important, but the actual content.** **Even less important, but the actual content.** **Even less important, but the actual content.** **Please, don't ignore me.** The superfine print, also not to be ignored.
Tree systems	This is the main design hierarchy of computer system file management. Where broad categories lead, in a linear fashion, to more specific, branching off as needed, getting ever more specific.	
Nest systems	This hierarchy maps information into clusters of primary, sub-primary, sub-sub-primary. This can go in multiple directions.	

CHAPTER 6: **Compositional Ideas and Design Principles**

Scale and Proportion

Scale and proportion in design can instantly make something grand or transcendent, or cute, human, and relatable. A city like Washington, D.C., is designed to have certain elements at grand scale, and others, like the street layout, in such a proportion to make the city an easy walk from grand building to grand building, making for a balance of scale and proportion.

A breakdown of scale and proportion is as follows:

Tool/Strategy	Definition	Image
Size	Similar objects at different sizes can create a sense of space, distance, and visual interest.	
Ratio	Object created on a given ratio (like the golden mean 1:1.618) make sense to the viewer, or user (paper sizes are derived from cutting down a larger sheet into common sizes, creating a ratio).	

Introduction to Digital Media for Designers and Artists

Part of the whole (divisions)	Using elements based on parts of larger elements gives a sense of organization.	

Dominance and Emphasis

We experience this design principle anytime we **bold** a word, or <u>underline</u> a sentence. Understanding dominance and emphasis is intuitive, but understanding its use effectively can be the difference between understanding and miscommunication; think about an inexperienced person typing in all caps on social media—do they mean what you think they mean?

Tool/Strategy	Definition	Image
Size	Obviously, the larger the element the more emphasis it could have	

CHAPTER 6: **Compositional Ideas and Design Principles**

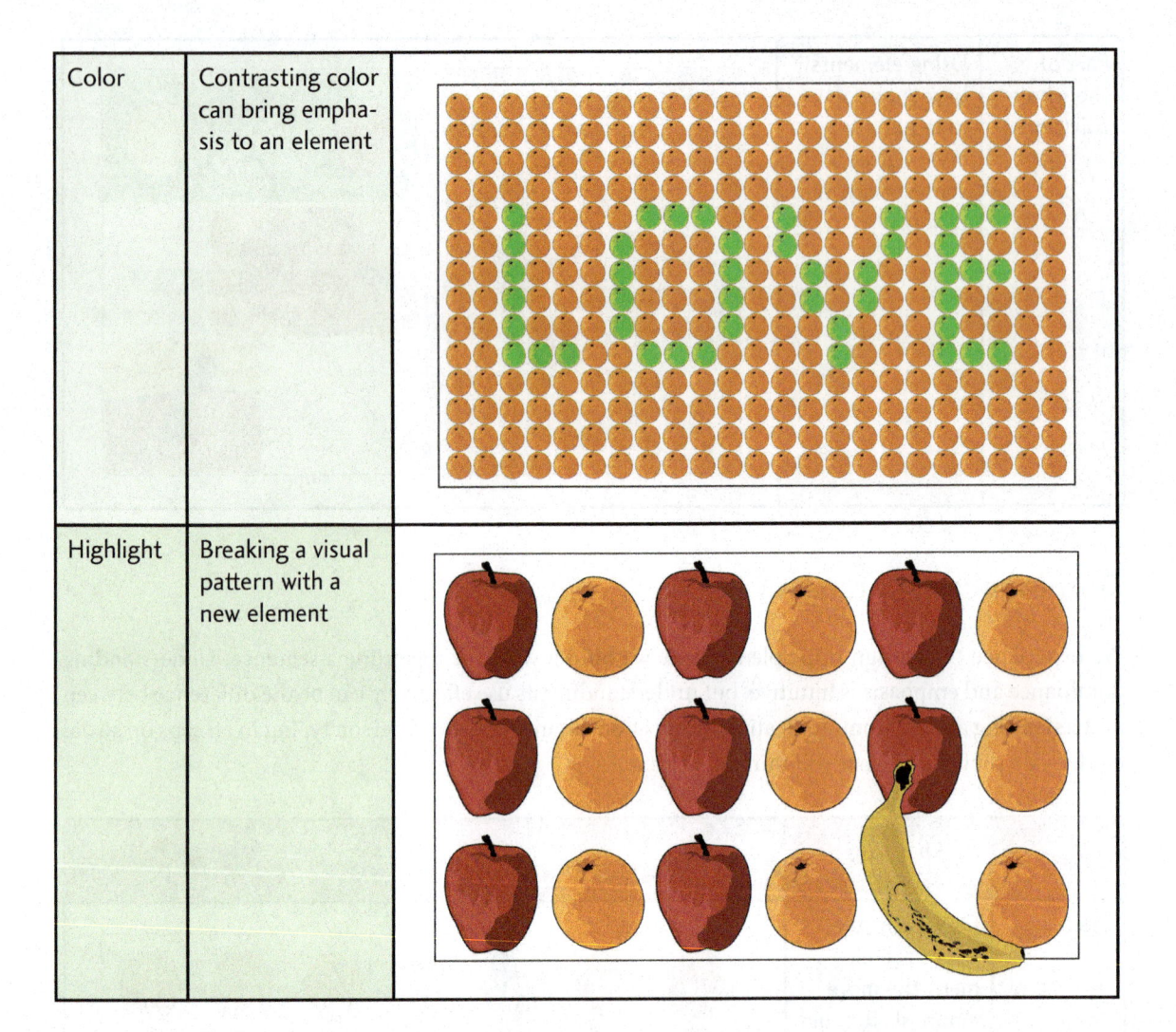

Color	Contrasting color can bring emphasis to an element	
Highlight	Breaking a visual pattern with a new element	

Introduction to Digital Media for Designers and Artists

Similarity and Contrast

Similarity and contrast reflect the discovery of elements in visual communication with enough variance to be compelling, but with enough distinction to avoid visual monotony.

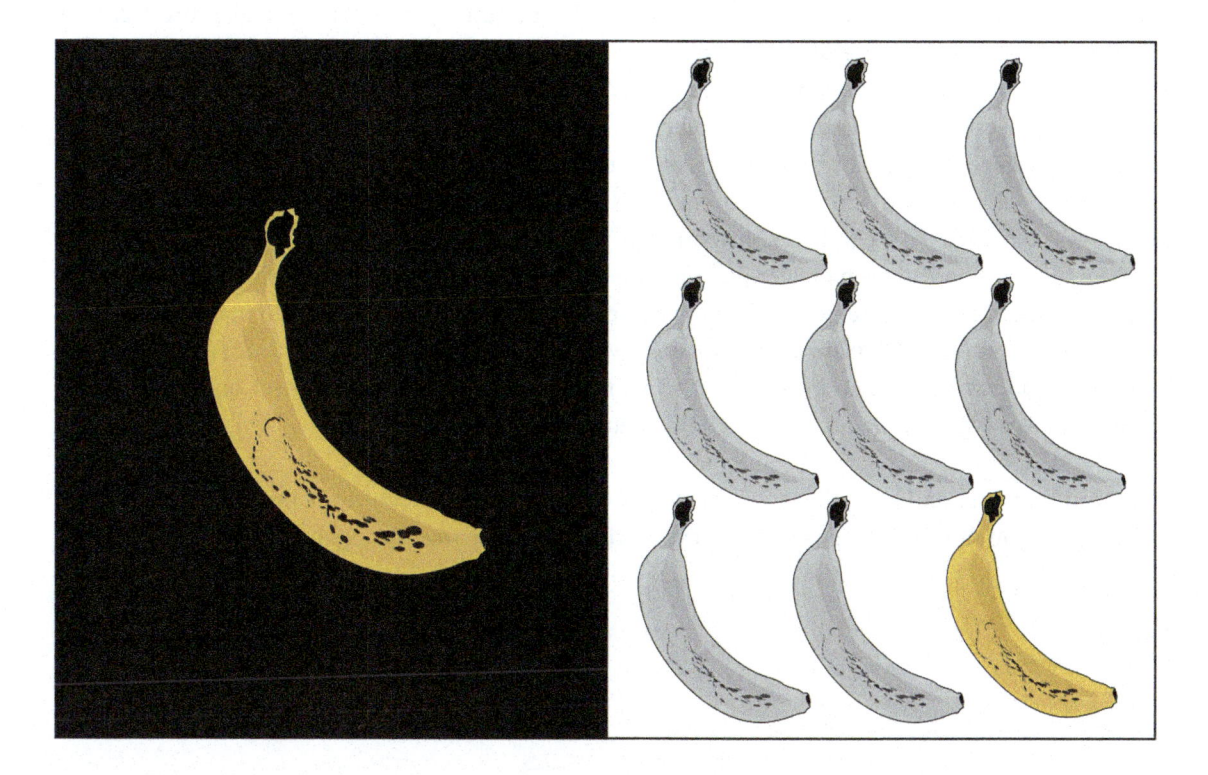

THOUGHTS ON RULES IN DESIGN AND ART

As we read through what is essentially a list of vocabulary for talking and thinking about visual communication, the rules overlap. This overlap reflects 40,000 years of human thought about the creation of visual images for art and graphic design—that is, visual communication. I want to make sure it is clear we, as makers of visual culture, should have our own thoughts on matters visual. This statement is not to give license to visual anarchy, or worse the "because I like it" syndrome, in which the only opinion of value is *yours*. We still need standards, general rules, active dialogue, and a sense of cultural and societal relevance when executing creative endeavors. But, we need to continually question this last 40 millennia, and the rules put forth by a generally eurocentric history of art and design. European art of the late 19th century was upended by the technical invention of photography, but one could argue trade and travel to Asia and Africa had an even greater influence on European art and design with the appropriation of art and design strategies of everything from Japanese woodcut prints to West African mask designs. The modern art movements of Europe would not exist without challenges mounted by artists and designers looking around the established tropes to other sources. I say this without comment on the wholesale appropriation of culture into fashion, which is a matter for discussion.

Clearly, make things and learn the language of your current aesthetic culture, be fluent but also critical, and awake as you draw this language, being ever vigilant of the changes being made by, for, and to you.

Helpful Information

We go through life as designers and artists needing to know so much information, hence the specialization of subfields: Print Designer, UX Designer, Front End Designer, Painter, Printmaker, Layout Designer, etc. I thought it would be nice to have just a few of these needed terms listed and explained. I know my students need this information all the time.

THE SIZE OF THINGS

Measurement Prefixes

We find these prefixes at work particularly when talking about file or storage device sizes, and when talking about bytes.

Prefix Name	Symbol	10ⁿ	Decimal	English
yotta	Y	10^{24}	1000000000000000000000000	sextillion
zetta	Z	10^{21}	1000000000000000000000	quintillion
exa	E	10^{18}	1000000000000000000	quadrillion
peta	P	10^{15}	1000000000000000	trillion
tera	T	10^{12}	1000000000000	billion
giga	G	10^{9}	1000000000	million
mega	M	10^{6}	1000000	thousand
kilo	k	10^{3}	1000	hundred
hecto	h	10^{2}	100	ten
deca	da	10^{1}	10	one
		10^{0}	1	tenth
deci	d	10^{-1}	0.1	hundredth
centi	c	10^{-2}	0.01	thousandth
milli	m	10^{-3}	0.001	millionth
micro	μ	10^{-6}	0.000001	billionth
nano	n	10^{-9}	0.000000001	trillionth
pico	p	10^{-12}	0.000000000001	quadrillionth
femto	f	10^{-15}	0.000000000000001	quintillionth
atto	a	10^{-18}	0.000000000000000001	sextillionth
zepto	z	10^{-21}	0.000000000000000000001	septillionth
yocto	y	10^{-24}	0.000000000000000000000001	sextillion

Paper

North American Paper Sizes

PAPER SIZE	INCHES	MILLIMETERS
Junior Legal	8 x 5	203 x 127
Government Letter	8 x 10.5	203 x 267
Letter	8.5 x 11	216 x 279
Legal	8.5 x 14	216 x 356
Tabloid	11 x 17	279 x 432
Ledger	17 x 11	432 x 279

B plus (Super B) has dimensions of 13" x 19" (329 mm x 483 mm).

International Paper Sizes

PAPER SIZE	MILLIMETERS	INCHES
A0	841 x 1189	33.110 x 46.811
A1	594 x 841	23.386 x 33.110
A2	420 x 594	16.535 x 23.386
A3	297 x 420	11.693 x 16.535
A4	210 x 297	8.268 x 11.693
A5	148 x 210	5.827 x 8.268
A6	105 x 148	4.134 x 5.827
A7	74 x 105	2.913 x 4.134
A8	52 x 74	2.047 x 2.913

SEARCH TERMS

Paper Sizes

CHAPTER 7: **Helpful Information**

Video

Viewing Device Standard Sizes

Standard	Aspect ratio	Width (px)	Height (px)	Name Meaning
CGA	4:3	320	240	Color Graphics Adaptor
VGA	4:3	640	480	Video Graphics Array (Standard TV resolution)
SVGA	4:3	800	600	Super Video Graphics Array
WSVGA	~17:10	1024	600	Wide Super Video Graphics Array
XGA	4:3	1024	768	Extended Graphics Array
XGA+	4:3	1152	864	Extended Graphics Array Plus
WXGA	16:9	1280	720	Wide Extended Graphics Array
WXGA	5:3	1280	768	Wide Extended Graphics Array
WXGA	16:10	1280	800	Wide Extended Graphics Array
SXGA	5:4	1280	1024	Super Extended Graphics Array
HD	~16:9	1360	768	High Definition
HD	~16:9	1366	768	High Definition
WXGA+	16:10	1440	900	Wide Extended Graphics Array Plus
HD+	16:9	1600	900	High Definition Plus
UXGA	4:3	1600	1200	Ultra Extended Graphics Array
WSXGA+	16:10	1680	1050	Widescreen Super Extended Graphics Array Plus
FHD	16:9	1920	1080	Full High Definition
WUXGA	16:10	1920	1200	Wide Ultra Extended Graphics Array
WQHD	16:9	2560	1440	Wide Quad High Definition
WQXGA	16:10	2560	1600	Wide Quad Extended Graphics Array
4K UHD	16:9	3840	2160	Ultra High Definition (4K is for 4 Kilo pixels, or 4,000 pixels referring to the width of the image—3,840 pixels)
8K UHD	16:9	7680	4320	Ultra High Definition (8,000 pixels)

> **NOTE**
>
> **Helpful Note on Resolution for Adobe Animate**
> If you are creating an animation and want to export it to full high definition (1920 x 1080), a good working stage size is 640 x 360, which is a 16:9 aspect ratio.

Video Shooting Resolutions

High-definition video modes

Video mode	Frame size in pixels (W×H)	Pixels per image	Scanning type	Frame rate (Hz)
720p	1280 × 720	921,600	Progressive	23.976, 24, 25, 29.97, 30, 50, 59.94, 60, 72
1080i	1920 × 1080	2,073,600	Interlaced	25 (50 fields/s), 29.97 (59.94 fields/s), 30 (60 fields/s)
1080p	1920 × 1080	2,073,600	Progressive	24 (23.976), 25, 30 (29.97), 50, 60 (59.94)
1440p	2560 × 1440	3,686,400	Progressive	24 (23.976), 25, 30 (29.97), 50, 60 (59.94)

Ultra high-definition video modes

Video mode	Frame size in pixels (W×H)	Pixels per image	Scanning type	Frame rate (Hz)
2000	2048 × 1536	3,145,728	Progressive	24
2160p (also known as 4k)	3840 × 2160	8,294,400	Progressive	60, 120
2540p	4520 × 2540	11,480,800	Progressive	
4000p	4096 × 3072	12,582,912	Progressive	
4320p (also known as 8k)	7680 × 4320	33,177,600	Progressive	60, 120

TYPOGRAPHY BASICS

As people who use computers and search the Internet, we understand type, fonts, and, to some degree, how type functions in our day-to-day lives. But the terms and the basic creation of fonts is a mystery; and the mastery of type use is an allusive goal. I hope this section will move you toward thinking about the type you use and notice some of the specifics of type design.

Font

A font is a group of characters with a level of cohesion to be recognized as being from the same root design idea. A full font contains all the letters, numbers, and other characters needed to dress language in that font. Different languages have different character sets. This leaves room for near limitless variety and variation. A font family will contain bold, italic (or oblique), sometimes light, extra light, heavy, extra bold, bold italic, etc. There are thousands if not millions of fonts, and hundreds if not thousands of font families. This can make choosing fonts very difficult.

SEARCH TERMS

Movable type, *Helvetica* (2007, film by Gary Hustwit), Massimo Vignelli, Wim Crouwel, Matthew Carter, Hermann Zapf, Michael Bierut, Tobias Frere-Jones, Jonathan Hoefler, Erik Spiekermann, Neville Brody, Paula Scher, Stefan Sagmeister, David Carson, Experimental Jetset, Michael C. Place, Norm

Typefaces go through a life of fashion, and fall into favor and out of favor, what looked good in some 20th-century typography looks goofy now, and so on. We create things for a time, or because of a time, and fonts play a very important role in defining time and place.

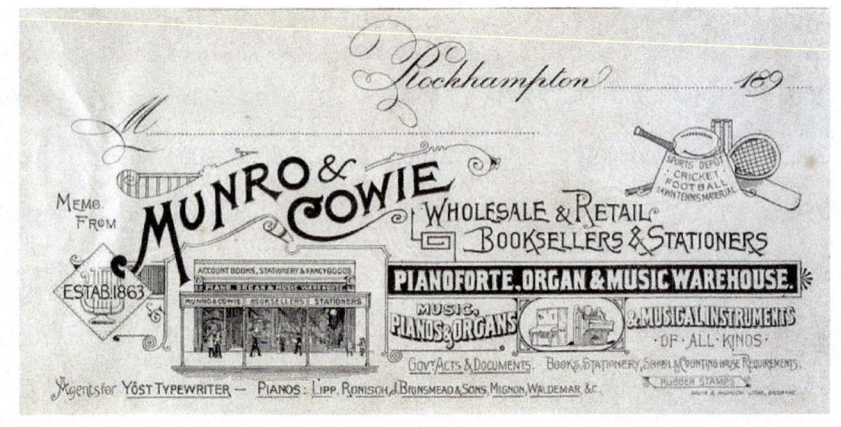

Courtesy State Library of Queensland

108 Introduction to Digital Media for Designers and Artists

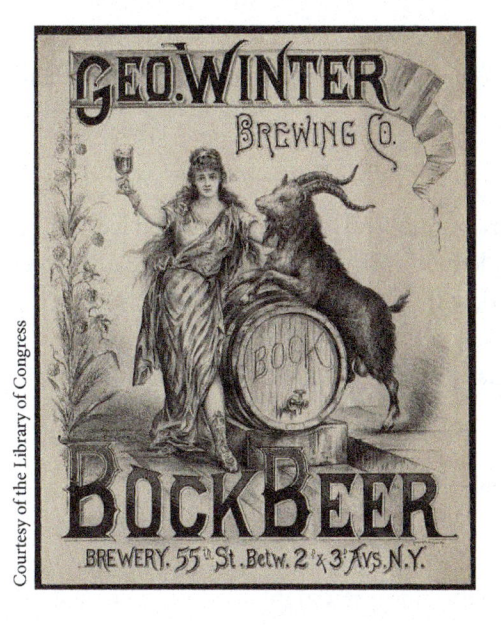

Now is the time for all great people to come to the aid of their country.

Serif Typeface Garamond Regular

Now is the time for all great people to come to the aid of their country.

Sans Serif Typeface Avenir Book

Fonts fall into two general categories, *serif* and *sans serif*. Serif fonts have serifs, the little spikes at the ends of the type. Sans serif fonts do not have serifs.

CHAPTER 7: Helpful Information

Classification of Some Serif Typefaces

Old-style: characterized by a lack of difference between the thick and thin parts of the characters. Some example fonts: Bembo, Berkeley Old Style, Caslon, Centaur, Cloister, Fairfield, Garamond, Galliard, Granjon, Goudy Old Style, Minion, Hightower Text, Janson, Legacy, Palatino, Renard, Sabon, Scala, and Trinité

Transitional, or *baroque*: characterized by having a balance between the thick and thin parts; not as similar as old-style, not as contrasting as modern typefaces. Transitional typefaces usually have a fancy curl on the capital Q. Some example fonts: Aurora, Baskerville, Bell, Bitstream Charter, Bookman, Bulmer, Caledonia, Cambria, Century (type family), Fournier MT, Georgia, Imprint, Liberation Serif, Mrs Eaves.

Modern, or *didone*: characterized by having a great deal of contrast between the thick and thin parts of the characters. Also, modern typefaces tend to have ball terminals on characters, like lowercase a, c, f, and j. Some example fonts: Didot, Ambicase Modern, Bodoni, Modern No. 20, and Scotch Modern.

Slab serif (also called *mechanistic*, *square serif*, *antique* or *Egyptian*): characterized by having blocky serifs, generally at right angles to the character. Some example fonts: Clarendon, Rockwell, Archer, Courier, Excelsior, FF Meta Serif, and Guardian Egyptian.

Latin or *wedge-serif:* characterized by having serifs that come to a point, like a wedge. Example fonts: Copperplate, PL Latin, Pescadero, and Latin 725.

Classification of Sans Serif Typefaces, Display Fonts, and Others
Sans serif fonts are classified as such. You will see the words "gothic" and "grotesk" (German for "gothic") used in the names of many sans serif fonts. Some example fonts: Helvetica, Futura, Gill Sans, Avenir, Frutiger, Univers, DIN, Avant Garde Gothic, Meta, Myriad, and Arial.

Display fonts are typefaces that defy category and are usually made for a special purpose, like an icicle font for a snowcone company, for example.

There are also handwriting fonts, calligraphy fonts, blackletter fonts, and symbol fonts.

Weight and Italic
A complete typeface will have an entire family of fonts with different weights and italics in different weights. Weight refers to how bold or light the font is. Italic refers to a slanted typeface, which is also called oblique. A full family will have a bold version of the italic face as well.

Typographic Size and Spacing

Typographic size is described in points and picas.

There are roughly 72 points to 1 inch (PostScript uses an exact 72 points to 1 inch).

There are roughly 6 picas to 1 inch (PostScript uses an exact 6 picas to 1 inch).

The following chart is in PostScript measurements:

Inch Factions	Inch Decimal	Picas	Points
⅛"	.125"	0p9	9pt
3/16"	.1875"	1p1.51	13.5pt
¼"	.25"	1p6	18pt
5/16"	.3125"	1p10.5	22.5pt
⅜"	.375"	2p3	27pt
7/16"	.4375"	2p7.5	31.5pt
½"	.5"	3p	36pt
9/16"	.5625"	3p4.5	40.5pt
⅝"	.625"	3p9	45pt
11/16"	.6875"	4p2.5	49.5pt
¾"	.75"	4p6	54pt
13/16"	.8125"	4p10.5	58.5pt
⅞"	.875"	5p3	63pt
15/16"	.9375"	5p7.5	67.5pt
1"	1.0"	6p	72pt

CHAPTER 7: Helpful Information

Generally, points are used for font size, and picas are used for page widths. Inches are also used for page dimensions in print, and the decision to use inches or picas is a personal one, unless it is specified; points are always used for type size in print. For the Web, all kinds of units are used but pixels are the native language of HTML, so pixels tend to be the unit most used.

Em and En Dashes

An em in typography is the width of a capital *M*, so an em dash (—) is the width of most capital *M*s, but since an *M* would generally be cut from a square, an em is equal to the point height of the font being used. An en is half of an em, so an en dash (–) is half the width of an em dash. In Web design *em* can be very handy for creating type sizes based on current or default type sizes, as 1 em is equal to the current set type size.

Parts of Type

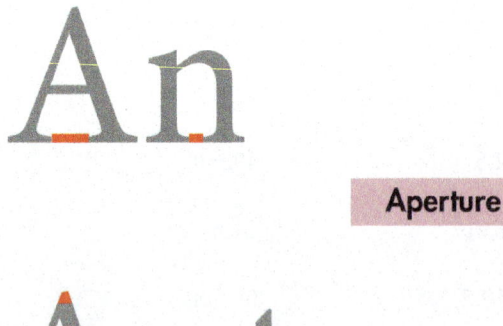

Aperture is the opening at the end of an open counter (the open space in a letter).

Apex is the peak or top of an uppercase *A*.

Introduction to Digital Media for Designers and Artists

End

Arm

Arm is a horizontal or diagonal stroke which does not connect to a stem on one or both ends (the top stroke on a capital *T* is an arm unconnected on both ends).

Dish

Ascender

Ascender is an upward vertical stroke extending above a font's x-height found on lowercase letters.

ELECT

Beak

Beak is similar to a spur, but projects from a straight stroke as in the ends of uppercase *L*, *T*, or *E*.

Base

Bowl

Bowl is a curved enclosing a letter's counter.

Art

Bracket or Fillet

Bracket (or **fillet**) is the curve connecting the serif to the stem or stroke of a letterform.

CHAPTER 7: **Helpful Information**

Oak

Counter

Counter is the partially or fully enclosed space within a letter (the open space on a partially enclosed counter is an aperture, on a capital *A* for example).

Hop

Crossbar

Crossbar is a horizontal stroke (unlike an arm, a crossbar is connected on both ends).

foot

Cross Stroke

Cross stroke is the horizontal part intersecting with the vertical part of a letterform as in *t* and *f*.

Fly

Descender

Descender is a downward vertical stroke extending below the baseline.

Arm

Diagonal Stroke

Diagonal stroke is an angled stroke.

Introduction to Digital Media for Designers and Artists

Pig

Ear

Ear is a small stroke projecting from some lowercase *g*s on the upper right of the bowl.

erect

Eye

Eye, similar to a counter, is the enclosed portion of a lowercase *e*.

Alive

Finial

Finial is a tapered or curved end on a letter lacking a serif (basically, an embellished terminal).

Rod

Hairline

Hairline is the thin part of the strokes of a serif typeface.

flute

Ligature

Ligature is a single glyph formed by joining two or more letters (this is only found with certain typefaces which have a full character set).

CHAPTER 7: Helpful Information

Gig
Link

Link is a stroke connecting the bowl and the loop of lowercase double-story *g*.

Wig
Loop

Loop is the enclosed or partially enclosed counter of a double-story *g* below the baseline.

Pill
Serif

Serif is the little "foot" or nonstructural detail at the end of some strokes.

hope
Shoulder

Shoulder is a curved stroke starting from a stem.

Sassy
Spine

Spine is the main curved stroke for an *S*, for both the capital and lowercase.

Gate

Spur

Spur is a small projection from a curved stroke.

Falt

Stem

Stem is the primary vertical stroke of a letter.

Raft

Tail

Tail is a descending stroke on a letter. It is often decorative as seen on certain letters Q, R, and K. The descender, especially if it is decorative, on letters g, j, p, q, and y are often referred to as tails.

from

Terminal

Terminal is the end of a stroke lacking a serif.

Typographic Positioning

Font size: the size of a font, in print this is in points. In Adobe applications this is set in the *Character* dialogue box, in Adobe Illustrator and InDesign *command (control) + t*.

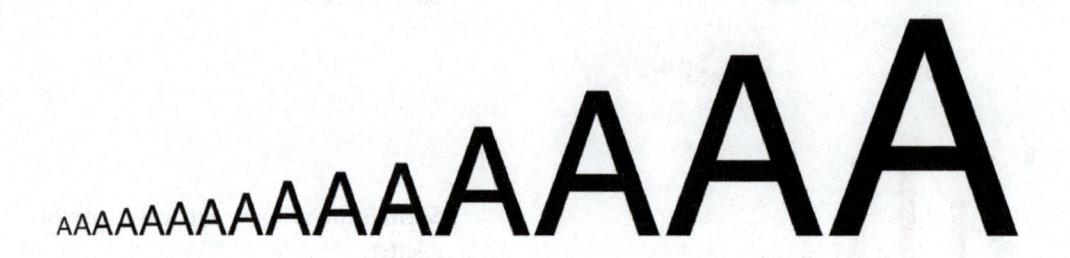

Font Weight: how thick or thin a particular font is in a font family. One would pick the bold or thin version of a particular font when setting type for publication. Adobe Illustrator and InDesign do not have a "bold" or "faux bold" function, assuming professionals use the real type specifications. Adobe Photoshop has a "faux bold" function in the Character menu. In CSS, use *font-weight: normal|bold|bolder|lighter|***number***|initial|inherit*.

Leading: the space between lines of text (also called line spacing). This measurement if from baseline to baseline. In Adobe applications, select type with the type tool, *hold option + (up or down) arrow-key*. In CSS, use *line-height:* property.

Now is the time for all great people to come to the aid of their country.

Now is the time for all great people to come to the aid of their country.

Now is the time for all great people to come

to the aid of their country.

Introduction to Digital Media for Designers and Artists

Tracking: the space between all the letters on a line of type (also called letter spacing). In Adobe applications, select type with the type tool, hold *hold option + (left or right) arrow-key*. In CSS, use *letter-spacing:* property (it can have a negative value).

> Now is the time for all great people to come to the aid of their country.
>
> Now is the time for all great people to come to the aid of their country.
>
> Now is the time for all great people to come to the aid of their country.

Kerning: the space between just two characters. In Adobe applications, place cursor with the type tool between two characters, hold *hold option + (left or right) arrow-key*. There is no real equivalent in CSS, but use of the *letter-spacing* property with great specificity can do the same thing.

> At this   At this

(Here we are looking at the space between the *A* and the *t*.)

Justification: the positioning of text in a paragraph or block. The common forms of justification are left, right, centered, and force or fully.

Lorem ipsum dolor sit amet, consectetur adipiscing elit. In non ipsum eget mauris consequat rutrum convallis eu erat. Cras ut ipsum quis quam posuere dictum et a nisi. Quisque id orci cursus, sagittis odio id, molestie tortor. Pellentesque eget tellus a neque suscipit euismod.

Lorem ipsum dolor sit amet, consectetur adipiscing elit. In non ipsum eget mauris consequat rutrum convallis eu erat. Cras ut ipsum quis quam posuere dictum et a nisi. Quisque id orci cursus, sagittis odio id, molestie tortor. Pellentesque eget tellus a neque suscipit euismod.

Lorem ipsum dolor sit amet, consectetur adipiscing elit. In non ipsum eget mauris consequat rutrum convallis eu erat. Cras ut ipsum quis quam posuere dictum et a nisi. Quisque id orci cursus, sagittis odio id, molestie tortor. Pellentesque eget tellus a neque suscipit euismod.

Lorem ipsum dolor sit amet, consectetur adipiscing elit. In non ipsum eget mauris consequat rutrum convallis eu erat. Cras ut ipsum quis quam posuere dictum et a nisi. Quisque id orci cursus, sagittis odio id, molestie tortor. Pellentesque eget tellus a neque suscipit euismod.

Lorem ipsum dolor sit amet, consectetur adipiscing elit. In non ipsum eget mauris consequat rutrum convallis eu erat. Cras ut ipsum quis quam posuere dictum et a nisi. Quisque id orci cursus, sagittis odio id, molestie tortor. Pellentesque eget tellus a neque suscipit euismod.

Lorem ipsum dolor sit amet, consectetur adipiscing elit. In non ipsum eget mauris consequat rutrum convallis eu erat. Cras ut ipsum quis quam posuere dictum et a nisi. Quisque id orci cursus, sagittis odio id, molestie tortor. Pellentesque eget tellus a neque suscipit euismod.

Lorem ipsum dolor sit amet, consectetur adipiscing elit. In non ipsum eget mauris consequat rutrum convallis eu erat. Cras ut ipsum quis quam posuere dictum et a nisi. Quisque id orci cursus, sagittis odio id, molestie tortor. Pellentesque eget tellus a neque suscipit euismod.

SEARCH TERMS

Typographic Alignment

There are many, many names for aligning type. You will need to be aware of the pictographic images in Adobe applications for the different types.

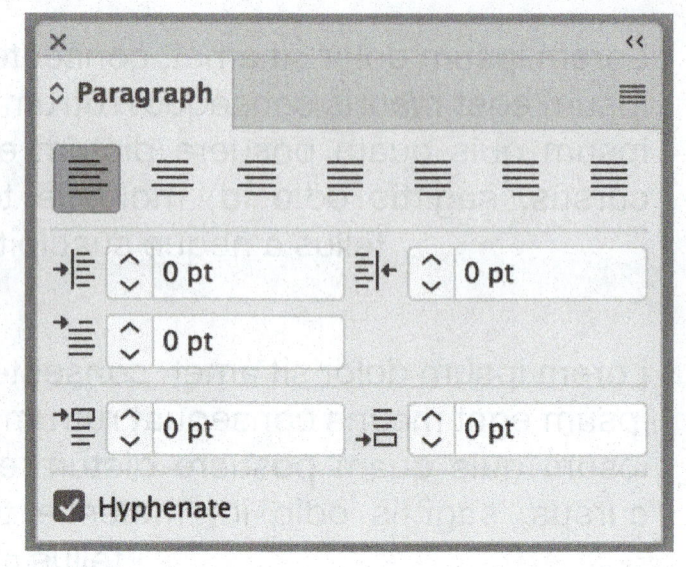

In CSS, use *text-align: left|right|center|-justify|initial|inherit;*. Note: The term *justify* leaves the last line of the block of text left-justified.

Grid Systems: It is essential you know about the idea of setting type, images, objects in designed grid systems. The mid-20th century brought an order to the systems of understanding of how type and image should function on a page. Then the late 20th century saw a revision, if not an outright overthrow of these ideas.

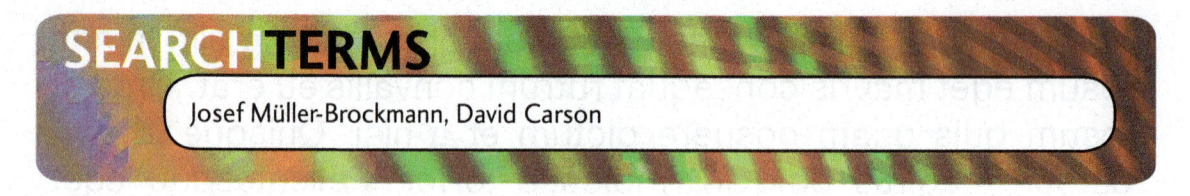

SEARCH TERMS

Josef Müller-Brockmann, David Carson

The side arguing for a system of rules and order, and grids, cites the ease of limits on the designer, as well as the visual order given to the viewer. The other side does not so much argue against rules as they argue to make their own rules. Designers and artists have always set up systems in which their creativity could function within known parameters. Grid systems give us known parameters. There is a design solution to be found, and grid systems are one way of finding it; but not the only way.

CHAPTER 7: Helpful Information

Title

Lorem ipsum dolor sit amet, consectetuer adipiscing elit, sed diam nonummy nibh euismod tincidunt ut laoreet dolore magna aliquam erat volutpat. Ut wisi enim ad minim veniam, quis nostrud exerci tation ullamcorper suscipit lobortis nisl ut aliquip ex ea commodo consequat. Duis autem vel eum iriure dolor in hendrerit in vulputate velit esse molestie consequat, vel illum dolore eu

"Breakout Text You Will Not Believe it!"

Lorem ipsum dolor sit amet, consectetuer adipiscing elit, sed diam nonummy nibh euismod tincidunt ut laoreet dolore magna aliquam erat volutpat. Ut wisi enim ad minim veniam, quis nostrud exerci tation ullamcorper suscipit lobortis nisl ut aliquip ex ea commodo consequat. Duis autem vel eum iriure dolor in hendrerit in vulputate velit esse molestie consequat, vel illum dolore eu feugiat nulla facilisis at vero eros et accumsan et iusto odio dignissim qui blandit praesent luptatum zzril delenit augue duis dolore te feugait nulla facilisi.

Lorem ipsum dolor sit amet, cons ectetuer adipiscing elit, sed diam nonummy nibh euismod tincidunt ut laoreet dolore magna aliquam erat volutpat. Ut wisi enim ad minim veniam, quis nostrud exerci tation ullamcorper suscipit lobortis nisl ut aliquip ex ea commodo consequat. Lorem ipsum dolor sit amet, consectetuer adipiscing elit, sed diam nonummy nibh euismod tincidunt ut laoreet dolore magna aliquam erat volutpat. Ut wisi enim ad minim veniam, quis nostrud exerci tation ullamcorper suscipit lobortis nisl ut aliquip ex ea commodo

Introduction to Digital Media for Designers and Artists

PRINTING

Most designers will have to know at least a little about printing. At the very least you are going to have to be able to follow the specifications to get business cards printed. As print designers and artists, having knowledge of printing processes and techniques will be invaluable. Here I have outlined just a few to light your way to more information.

Specifications (Spec)

Every printer will have specifications for a particular job. These could include:

Gutter margin: How close to the edge you can safely design, in order for your work not to get trimmed when cut to size, or get left too far into the binding on multipage projects.

Bleed margin: How far over the edge of the work you need to leave an image so it will go edge-to-edge, even after the piece is trimmed to size.

Other specifications: File format, file size, resolution (print is generally 300 dpi), color depth; are there color managed colors?

Resolution

Dots per inch (dpi), or pixels per inch (ppi): Simply, how many dots of ink we will have per inch to create our image. The standard is 300 dpi, but sometimes you will find just black printed as high as 1,200 dpi; one would never go below 150 dpi.

Printing Methods

Relief: Ink is rolled on the surface of a plate which has some higher and lower surfaces, the ink covers only the higher surfaces, and this is what is transferred to the paper or substrate.

Examples are Japanese (especially *ukiyo-e*) and Western woodblock printing, letterpress printing, flexography, and rubber stamps.

Utagawa Hiroshige, *Naruto Whirlpool*

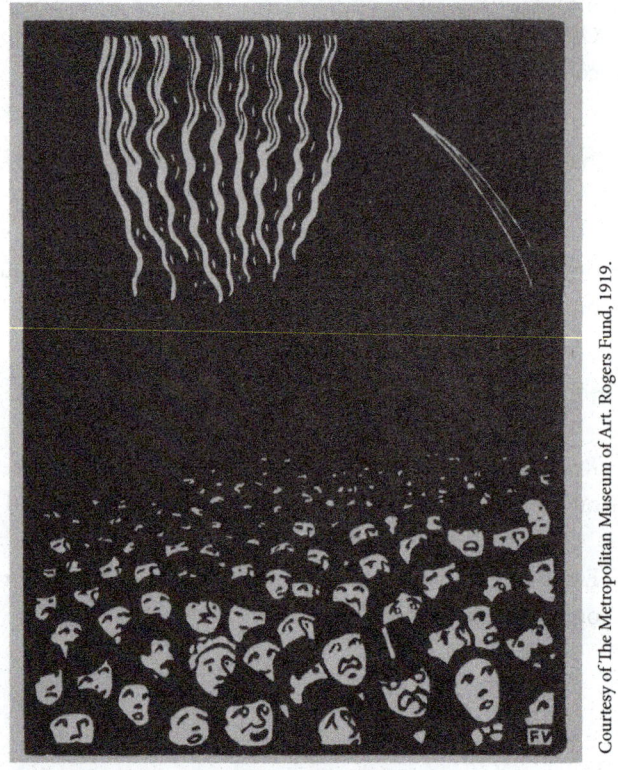

Félix Vallotton, *Fireworks, The World's Fair VI*

Introduction to Digital Media for Designers and Artists

Intaglio (gravure, etching, aquatint, mezzotint, engraving): Ink is wiped into spaces cut or etched (with acid) into a plate, leaving the ink in the "lines" (lower spaces), and under great pressure the ink is transferred from the lowered spaces onto the paper or substrate.

Enea Vico, *Rhinoceros*

CHAPTER 7: Helpful Information

Examples: fine art etching and engraving, and U.S. paper money.

Lithography (stone lithography, offset printing, waterless lithography): A part of a stone (mostly Bavarian limestone), or plate is chemically sensitized to favor oil, while the other parts are sensitized to favor water. When an oil-based ink is rolled over a moistened stone or plate, the ink attaches itself to the oil-sensitized parts, then paper or substrate is placed over the image, and transferred with pressure. In an offset process, this same process occurs, but instead of the image being transferred directly it is first printed on a rubber roller and then offset onto the paper or substrate. This allows the matrix (the plate or stone) to remain stationary, and for a stack of paper to be printed on at very high speeds. The other added benefit is the designer and press workers can see the image on the matrix right-way round, while in a traditional print the matrix is reverse-image (mirror image) from the print. Technological advances have allowed lithographic processes on aluminum plates, plastic plates, and waterless on other materials.

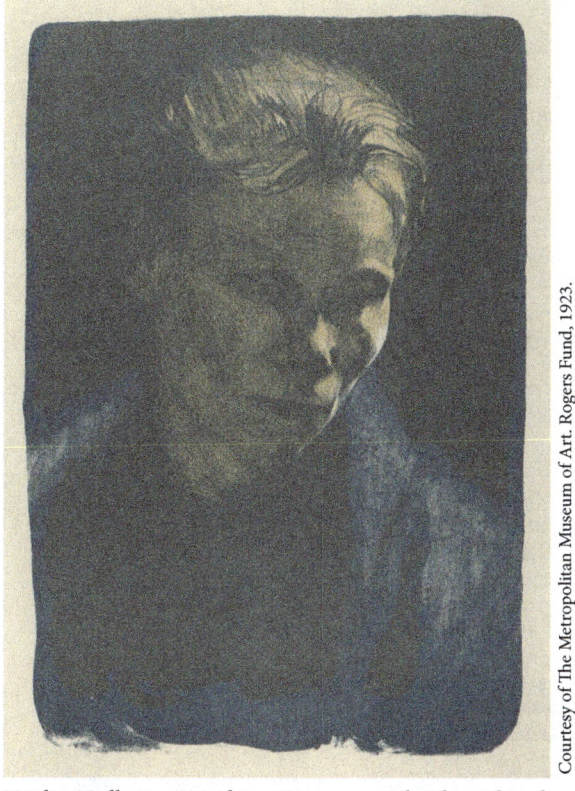

Käthe Kollwitz, *Working Woman with Blue Shawl*

Examples: fine art lithographs, books, magazines, catalogues.

Screen printing (silkscreen, serigraphy): A mesh screen is stretched on a frame, then the screen is blocked or left open. Ink is then squeegeed over the screen. Where the screen is open, ink passes through onto the material being printed, transferring the image or at least one color of the image. Generally, the screens are made photomechanically with a light-hardening emulsion and a black-and-white positive.

Examples: fabrics, t-shirts, fine art prints and posters.

CHAPTER 7: Helpful Information

SEARCH TERMS

Search terms for other types of printing: Dye Sublimation, Inkjet Printing (Giclée printing), Thermographic Printing, Xerography (electrostatic, laser printing)

WEB DESIGN

When it comes to Web design, I am going to put forward a few ideas and terms I have found useful in my experience in learning and teaching.

Setup

Before you begin a Web project, create a folder. This will be your *main*, *root*, or *local* folder. **All** your files will go into this folder, and into **no other** folders anywhere else.

I have a suggested setup, which seems to work well for art and design students.

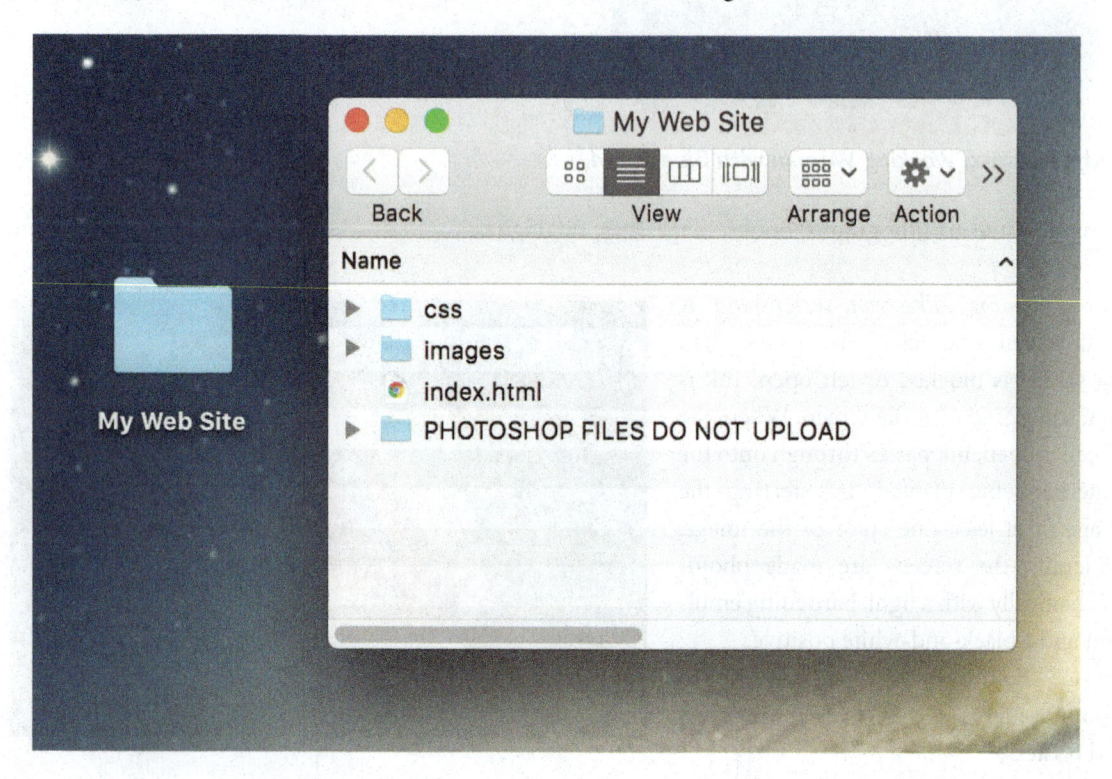

Introduction to Digital Media for Designers and Artists

This basic setup root folder (*My Web Site*), with *images*, *css*, and a *PHOTOSHOP DO NOT UPLOAD* folder inside, will give you a basic starting point. You will notice I also have an HTML file entitled *index.html*. Most website hosting companies use *index.html* as the default (starting) page to your website, so I always have students start with *index.html* as their first page. You will also notice the *PHOTOSHOP DO NOT UPLOAD* folder. I like to encourage my students to keep all their files in one place, but I do not want them to upload their master Photoshop or other image files to the server, wasting valuable upload time.

When naming HTML files only use standard alphanumeric characters (a–z, 0–9) and underscores (_) or dashes (-).

And always know where your files are.

Code Is Easy Speaking

When learning or writing HTML (Hyper Text Markup Language), and CSS (Cascading Style Sheets), the basic languages of Web pages, the most important thing to learn is the syntax—that is, the order of how the language is written and understood by the browser. In written English we understand a sentence to have a subject, a verb, and a complete thought. HTML and CSS also have set structures, but unlike human languages this structure is more rigid and defined, making it easier to learn. The "hard" part comes in knowing the vocabulary to fill in the structure, and in knowing what it is capable of or you are "allowed" to do with the language; these can easily be looked up on the Internet.

HTML Is Like Sandwiches inside Sandwiches

HTML is like a sandwich, in that for most of its phrasing it begins with an opening tag and closes with a closing tag, and these are surrounded by opening and closing tags—like the bread of a sandwich. The designers of HTML also used a typical biological system as the model for the primary structure of a Web page, with *<html>* containing a *<head>* and a *<body>* as the tags to create the page, with the *<body>* being what you see and the *<head>* telling it what to "do."

Basic HTML5 page:

<!DOCTYPE html>	*<!DOCTYPE html>* This defines the kind of html you are using
<html>	*<html>* This is the open tag starting the HTML
<head>	*<head>* This is the open tag starting the *head* of the document (page)
<title>Page Title</title>	
</head>	*<title>* This is the open tag for the page title—the title appears in the tab of the window
<body>	
	</title> This is the close tag for the page title; a "/" indicates the close for a given tag
This is what you see!	
	</head> This is the close tag for the page head
</body>	*<body>* This is the open tag for the *body*—the *body* contains the visible information on the page
</html>	
	</body> This is the close tag for the *body*
	</html> This closes the HTML document (page)

This basic form for HTML5 does not change, and is the basis of all contemporary Web pages.

CSS Tells HTML What to Look Like

Cascading Style Sheets (CSS) is a language which tells HTML what to look like. It has a very simple structure, with a vocabulary extensive enough to make HTML look just about any way you want it.

The structure of CSS in the *<head>*:

`<!DOCTYPE html>`
`<html>`
`<head>`
`<title>CSS Structure</title>`
 	
`<style type="text/css">`
 	
`body {`
`        background-color:blue;`
`}`
 	
`</style>`
`</head>`
`<body>`
`This page is blue`
`</body>`
`</html>`
	<style> This opens the *style* tag
	type="text/css" This tells the browser how you are inputting the information, and it is contained within the *<style>* tag, `<style type="text/css">`
	
	body This indicates which part of the HTML we are changing (this is referred to as the Selector). This functions as the *if* body *then*...
	
	{ This is an open curly bracket, which functions as the *then* part of an *if (then)* statement:
	
	background-color This is the property to be changed. *If* body *({) then change* background-color *(:) equal to* blue *(;) period or stop (}) end changes to body.*
	
	: This acts as a *to*, *is*, or *equal*
	
	blue This changes the background color of the page to blue, also written in hexadecimal as *#0000FF*, or in RGB as *rgb(0,0,255)*
	
	; This acts as a *period (.)* or a *stop* to the line
	
	} This closes the statement and the changes to *<body>*

Quick Start Example of a Web Page for Designers and Artists

Using block elements with dimension (in pixels), I am going to lay out a very basic page. I am including *background-color:* in all elements so you can see them as distinct elements, not as an aesthetic choice.

I am using *id* for the unique elements, and *class* for the typographic and other elements.

CHAPTER 7: **Helpful Information**

```html
<!doctype html>
<html>
<head>
<title>Basic Web Page for Artists and Designers</title>
<style type="text/css">
    body {
        background-color:#CCC;
        font-family: Gotham, "Helvetica Neue", Helvetica, Arial, "sans-serif";
        font-size: 14px;
    }
    div#centerHolder {
        height: 600px;
        width: 900px;
        background-color: rgba(255,0,0,0.1);
        margin: 0 auto;
    }
    div#titleHolder {
        height: 50px;
        width: 900px;
        position: absolute;
        margin-top: 0;
        background-color: lightblue;
        text-align: center;
        
    }
    .titleFont {
        font-family: Gotham, "Helvetica Neue", Helvetica, Arial, "sans-serif";
        font-size: 40px;
        font-weight: bold;
    }
    nav {
        height: 200px;
        width: 120px;
        position: absolute;
        margin:120px 20px;
        padding:5px;
        background-color: lightcoral;
    }
    ul {
        list-style: none;
        background-color: orangered;
    }
    li {
        padding:2px 0px 2px 5px;
        background-color: rgba(255,255,255,0.5);
    }
/*  This is how you write a CSS comment: slash-star and end with star-slash    */
    /* comments are used to make notes, and to turn elements off */
    div#contentHolder {
        height: auto;
        /*height:420px;*/
        width: 620px;
        position: absolute;
        margin-top: 120px;
        margin-left: 200px;
        padding:0 10px 0 10px;
        background-color: cadetblue;
    }
    img.roomAround {
        float: left;
        margin: 10px 10px 5px 0;
    }
    p.ParaJust {
        text-align: justify;
        line-height: 20px;
    }
```

134

Introduction to Digital Media for Designers and Artists

Notes:
Setting the font-family: in the body sets the font for the whole page.

#FFFFFF is how color is set in hexadecimal code with A–F and 0–9, with each paired set representing red, green, and blue respectively, so *#FF0000* is red, *#00FF00* is green, and *#0000FF* is blue. One can shorthand this by just using three places: *#CCC* is grey, *#FFF* is white, and *#000* is black.

CSS understands many different units so one must use px for pixels. CSS understands: *cm* (centimeters), *mm* (millimeters), *in* (inches), *pt* (points), and *pc* (picas), as well as *em* (em) and % (percent)—and others (search term: CSS units).

rgb(red,green,blue); and rgba(red,green,blue,alpha); is another way of describing color in CSS, with values between 0 and 255, and an alpha (how transparent) from 0.0 to 1.0 (with 1.0 being opaque). White would be *rgba(255,255,255,1.0)*, black, *rgba(0,0,0,1.0)*.

A *div* makes a rectangle # indicates a variable name for an id. In order to position the *div* it must have dimensions, height and width.

HTML also understands some named colors (search: HTML color names list); there are 140 of them.

Margin: *0 auto*; will center a <div> as the central holding rectangle. Meaning: it contains all the other elements between its <div> and </div> tags.

Note: " 0 " does not need a unit type, but I include them sometimes to be consistent (the code has some 0px to show it is okay to include).

position: absolute; tells the element to position itself exactly to the margins, disregarding the order of the elements. This also allows one to "stack" elements with *z-index*: a number; which will order the elements atop each other.

.NameVarible names a class, the (.) is used in CSS to indicate this. Hence, (.) for class and (#) for id. id is unique (only one) per page, class can be on multiple elements and can be compounded; example, <span class="wildFont redFont boldFont">Some wild red bold text</span>.

Comments in CSS and HTML—and all computer languages—are used to turn elements "off" and to leave clues as to what the writer did, for oneself and others. In CSS: /* to start, and */ to stop. In HTML: <!-- to start, and --> to stop.

Single properties with multiple values, like padding and margin. If the property has four values: *margin: 10px 5px 15px 100px;* top margin is 10px, right margin is 5px, bottom margin is 15px, left margin is 100px.

```
            img.rightFloat {
                float: right;
                margin-left: 10px;
            }
            footer {
                height: 17px;
                width:895px;
                position: absolute;
                margin-top: 580px;
                background-color: rgba(39,89,233,0.5);
                padding-left: 5px;
                padding-top: 3px;
                font-size: 11px;
            }
        </style>
    </head>
    <body>
    <div id="centerHolder">
            <div id="titleHolder"><span class="titleFont">My First Web Page</span></div>
        <!--            HTML comments are written like this:  lessThan-exclamation point-dash-dash and end with dash-dash-greaterThan      -->
                <nav>
                    <div style="text-align: center">Navigation Menu</div>
                    <ul>
                            <li><a href="#">Page 2</a></li>
                            <li><a href="#">Page 3</a></li>
                            <li><a href="#">Page 4</a></li>
                            <li><a href="#">Page 5</a></li>
                            <li><a href="#">Page 6</a></li>
                            <li><a href="#">Page 7</a></li>
                            <li><a href="#">Page 8</a></li>
                    </ul>
                </nav>
                <div id="contentHolder"><img src="images/cloud.png" height="162" width="100" alt="there would be an image in here" class="roomAround"><p>Here is my content</p>

                    <p>Lorem ipsum dolor sit amet, consectetur adipiscing elit. Aenean aliquet nec tellus id finibus. Nullam egestas consequat lorem, nec molestie dolor. Vestibulum sit amet libero diam. Vivamus ut sem magna. Sed a pharetra massa, et aliquam lacus. Suspendisse sed rutrum erat, vestibulum vestibulum erat. In nec neque ac leo mattis lacinia. Suspendisse at justo iaculis, pellentesque sapien ac, sollicitudin ex. Pellentesque et eleifend justo. Fusce mattis, purus id iaculis fringilla, neque nunc venenatis neque, et feugiat tellus augue efficitur purus. Etiam laoreet vehicula tortor nec finibus. Praesent sollicitudin enim et facilisis mollis. Phasellus blandit arcu sit amet suscipit molestie. Sed sed ante at massa luctus scelerisque sit amet sit amet ipsum. Proin quam neque, vulputate at leo non, efficitur lobortis massa.</p>

                    <p class="ParaJust"><img src="images/cloud.png" width="100" height="162" class="rightFloat" >Cras et efficitur dolor, quis volutpat quam. Aenean lacinia odio sit amet gravida fermentum. Phasellus dictum tincidunt justo, sit amet semper nunc finibus nec. Donec ornare bibendum interdum. Donec feugiat laoreet risus id fringilla. Quisque quis varius felis. Praesent convallis metus rhoncus ultricies tincidunt. Aliquam eros lacus, tincidunt ut tempus ac, eleifend a nisl. Nullam at diam viverra, consectetur lacus id, convallis ligula. Quisque facilisis nunc ut nunc blandit sagittis. Quisque vel vehicula erat, id bibendum risus. Cras gravida tempor porttitor. Donec auctor molestie metus sed imperdiet.</p>



            </div>

            <footer>Here are the credits to my site &copy; 2017</footer>

    </div>
    </body>
    </html>
```

If the margin property has three values: *margin: 15px 50px 10px;* top margin is 15px, right and left margins are 50px, bottom margin is 10px.

If the margin property has two values: *margin: 20px 30px;* top and bottom margins are 20px, right and left margins are 30px.

Setting a value to *auto* will expand the property to fit the content, or with *margin* (under certain conditions) it will center the object left-to-right.

float: left or *right*, is used to move an element to the left or right and allow other elements to fill in around it. In this case the text moves to the top of the image, not treating it like it is on the same baseline as it would without the *float*.

ul is an unordered list, and *li* is a list item. I used *list-style:none;* in order to remove the default bulletpoints.

nav in HTML5 is used to specify your navigation box without having to assign an *id* name.

<div style="text-align: center;"> Is a way to write CSS inline using style="" in a general *<div>* tag.

To link to another page in the same folder as your page: *<a href="your_page.html">*. To link to a page on the Internet: *<a href="http://www.something-something.com">*.

<img src="images/cloud.png" height="162" width="100"> is the code used to place an image from a folder images named cloud.png into your page (Note: the link to *images/cloud.png* is only on my system, if you paste the code the image link will be broken.)

Note: The fill-text is Lorem Ipsum (search: *Lorem Ipsum*) and is used to fill space with text.

footer in HTML5 is the name for the box holding the information at the bottom of the page, again without using an *id* name.

© inserts a copyright symbol, HTML uses &___; to display characters and symbols, either not on a normal keyboard or will be confusing to HTML, for example an ampersand (&) is written *&* and nondirectional quotation marks are created with *"* (search: HTML symbols).

CHAPTER 7: Helpful Information

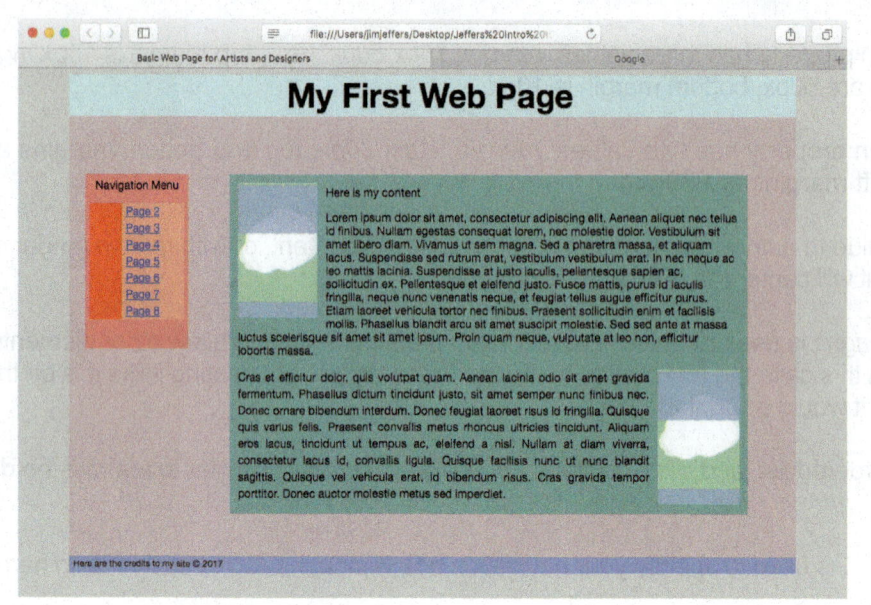

I would not expect this information to really be enough to become a full-fledged Web designer, but I would hope it might peek some curiosity.

SEARCH TERMS

Search terms with short explanations:
DOM: Document Object Model
HTML: Hypertext Markup Language: The simple language used to write Web pages
CSS: Cascading Style Sheets: The simple language used to format the look and layout of Web pages
JavaScript: The scripting language used to make rich interaction for the Web
URL: uniform resource locator
UX: user experience
UI: user interface
IA: information architecture
Interaction Design
PHP: personal homepage: A language used to enrich HTML by interfacing with a database
MySQL: my structured query language: A database language used in conjunction with PHP to create interactive, searchable, responsive database driven websites
jQuery: A shorthand JavaScript interface for designers allowing rich media creation for websites with limited coding
AJAX: asynchronous JavaScript and XML

More search terms: Drupal, Joomla, Squarespace, Weebly, WordPress, w3schools.com